FLATS: TECHNICAL DRAWING FOR FASHION

A Complete Guide

SECOND EDITION

LAURENCE KING

LAURENCE KING PUBLISHING LTD
361–373 City Road, London,
EC1V 1LR, United Kingdom
T +44 20 7841 6900
F +44 20 7841 6910
enquiries@laurenceking.com
www.laurenceking.com

ISBN: 978 1 78067 837 5

TEXT BY Basia Szkutnicka

TECHNICAL DRAWINGS BY
Ana Stankovic-Fitzgerald

DESIGN BY The Urban Ant

COVER DESIGN BY
Jane Chipchase-Bates

TOILES CREATED BY Anne Stafford

SENIOR EDITOR Gaynor Sermon

Printed in China

A step-by-step Illustrator tutorial is
available to view on the Laurence King
website, together with downloadable
figure templates and basic garment
styles. www.laurenceking.com.

FLATS: TECHNICAL DRAWING FOR FASHION

A Complete Guide

SECOND EDITION

BASIA SZKUTNICKA

LAURENCE KING PUBLISHING

Contents

A step-by-step Illustrator tutorial is available to view on the Laurence King website, together with downloadable figure templates and basic garment styles. www.laurenceking.com.

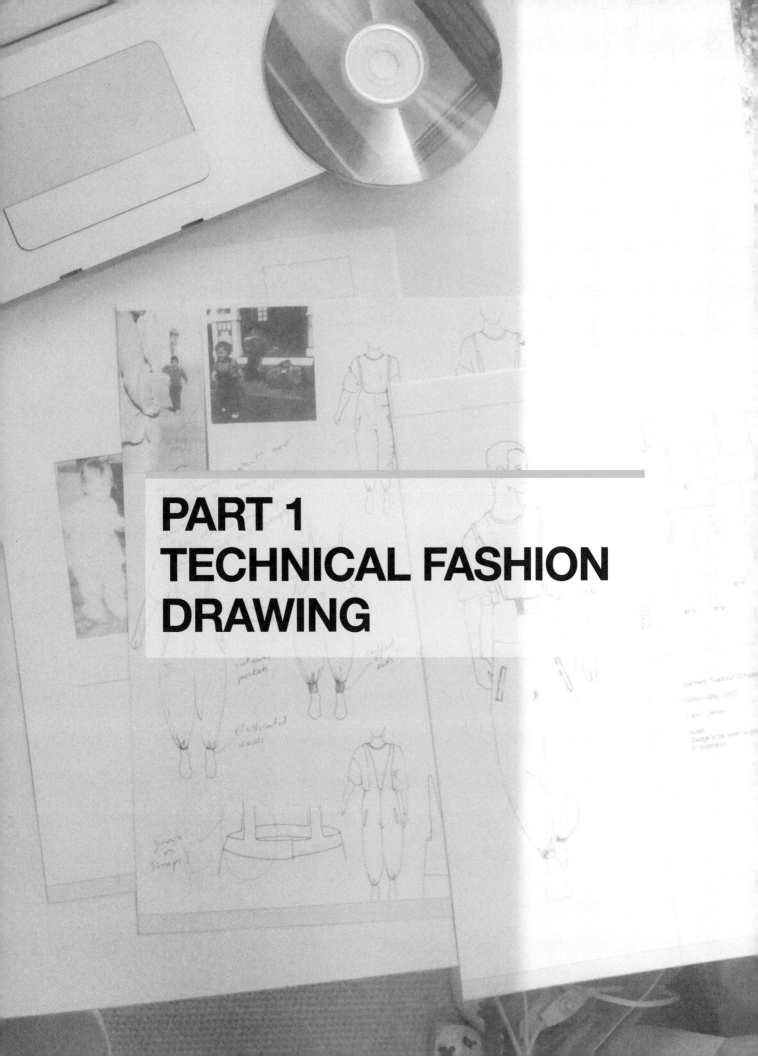

PART 1
TECHNICAL FASHION
DRAWING

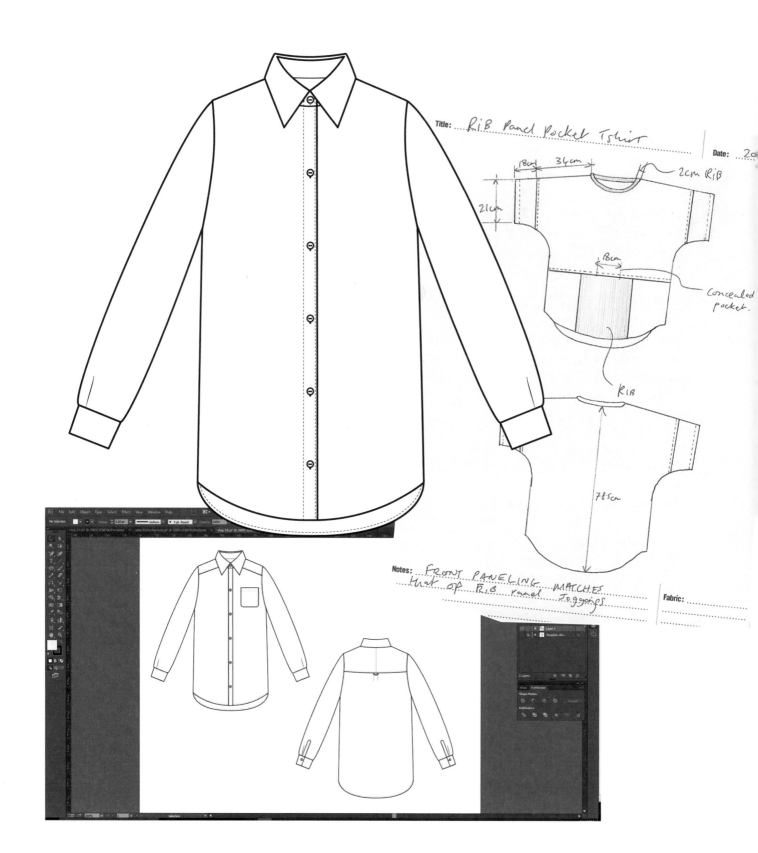

Title: Rib Panel Pocket Tshirt

Date: 20

2cm Rib

18cm 34cm

21cm

18cm

Concealed pocket.

RIB

78.5cm

Notes: FRONT PANELING MATCHES that of RIB panel Joggings

Fabric:

Introduction

The ability to produce technical drawings, or flats, is a necessary skill in the fashion industry. Flats are used to convey a design idea and all its construction details to anyone involved in the production process. They are also an effective way of communicating silhouette, proportion, and detail. Differently adapted flats are used for line boards, costings, specifications, paper patterns, look books, fashion forecasting, and online retail.

With production being sourced from a host of international locations, any means that can be found to overcome language and skill barriers can provide a very effective way of speeding up the production process and eliminating errors caused by misunderstandings. Drawing offers a universal means of communication, a visual language to facilitate this.

This book shows how to communicate your design ideas using technical drawing. The technique demonstrated starts with the creation of a generic body template, which can then be adapted and used to create flats. This can be done by hand or using CAD, or a combination of the two. Both hand-drawn and CAD methods are shown in the book, the latter demonstrated using Adobe Illustrator. The aim is to convey basic information and demonstrate a skill, rather than to teach a drawing style. However, no two people's flats will be exactly alike and there is room to develop your own personal style.

The techniques demonstrated will result in flats that can be used

and understood across all branches/sectors/stages of the fashion industry. This simple step-by-step method can also be used as part of the creative design process. Using a technique called "speed designing" you will see how, once a garment template has been drawn, it can be used as inspiration for an almost limitless range of garment shapes and details.

A fundamental requirement for fashion design is a sound knowledge of the basics: understanding key garment styles and their construction will enable you to develop and design endless variations. The second part of this book presents a visual directory of classic garment shapes and their variations, plus key garment styling and details. The basic styles are presented as a muslin photographed on a mannequin alongside a technical drawing, so that you can see how a three-dimensional shape translates into a two-dimensional, or flat, drawing.

Armed with this basic information, and following the step-by-step method, you will be able to create your own templates—or utilize those provided—to produce your own finished garment designs, while developing your own unique style of drawing. In this second edition many of the drawings have been updated to reflect the new templates on pages 20-25. The Illustrator tutorial has also been expanded, and a new section on knitwear added.

Drawing as part of the fashion process

Technical drawing is one of the methods used in the design process to present a garment in a visual format. The others are sketching and fashion illustration. Each has a specific function and thus demands a specific set of drawing requirements and techniques.

SKETCHING

A sketch is a rough, spontaneous drawing that is not necessarily accurate or even in proportion. It is the beginning of an idea, the inspiration. You can sketch from your imagination, from an existing style, or from reference. If you are producing store reports, or gathering field information, the aim is to note down a rough interpretation of a garment with key details that can be deciphered easily at a later stage if required.

Part of design development, the sketching process is when you let your imagination run riot, investigating sources of inspiration and abstract themes. It is the stage when you can work freely and experiment, thinking on paper. Usually produced by hand, the sketches can be drawn using any media.

FASHION ILLUSTRATION

The aim of a fashion illustration is to seduce and enhance, rather than provide technical information. Apparel is often illustrated on the figure to give an idea of a garment's proportions and how it will look when worn. Fashion illustrations are used in advertising, magazines, brochures, pattern books, and promotional material. A successful illustration will show mood, attitude, silhouette, proportion, and color to assist in the marketing of the garment. Its aim is to sell individual garments or to promote a brand.

Possessing emotion, energy, flair, creativity, and often movement, the fashion illustration allows the illustrator artistic freedom to inject their own personality into the drawing. With this freedom comes the artistic license to alter the proportions of the female body. Traditionally, the proportion of the female figure in fashion illustration is measured in heads, where the height of the figure can be calculated by dividing the length of the body by the height of the head. Fashion illustration typically elongates the female form to a proportion of nine to ten heads, resulting in a visually pleasing slender image, in contrast to the true average female height of approximately seven and a half heads.

Fashion illustrations today are created using a wide variety of media, ranging from traditional artistic materials to 2D and even 3D CAD (computer-aided design) software.

FLATS

Flats are a form of visual communication and instruction between the designer and the manufacturer, between the designer and buyer, and between the designer and a lay person. They are widely used throughout the apparel industry, in the design room (for design development and on line boards), in production (on costing and specification sheets), in marketing (in look books and on price lists), and in online retail.

Also known as "working drawings" or "line drawings," technical drawings are an accurate representation of a garment without a figure, summarizing styling details and showing construction, including construction lines, stitching, and decorative trims and details. They are drawn to scale, symmetrical, and in perfect proportion. Accurate flats are usually produced once a design has been finalized, and may be produced by hand or using CAD software.

How and when are flats used?

Flats, as we have already seen, have a variety of uses. Both students and designers in industry can use them in design development, when they can be drawn by hand, while CAD comes into its own for drawings destined for line boards and display presentation. Noted on the following pages are their key uses both within a learning environment and in industry.

Flats created for presentation sheets, development sheets, line boards and sheets, look books, and price lists can be injected with the illustrator's personality. Different pen widths can be used and a variety of line introduced to make them more interesting and aesthetically appealing, though this must be done without compromising on detail.

For specification sheets and costing sheets, however, the drawing needs to be completely accurate and more diagrammatic in character.

PRESENTATION SHEETS AND DESIGN DEVELOPMENT SHEETS FOR THE STUDENT

When studying fashion design, flats may be used alongside sketches and illustrations to clarify construction information and to communicate proportion.

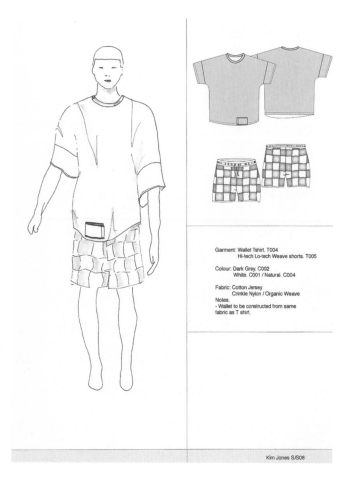

Garment: Wallet Tshirt. T004
Hi-tech Lo-tech Weave shorts. T005

Colour: Dark Grey. C002
White. C001 / Natural. C004

Fabric: Cotton Jersey
Crinkle Nylon / Organic Weave
Notes.
- Wallet to be constructed from same
fabric as T shirt.

Kim Jones S/S06

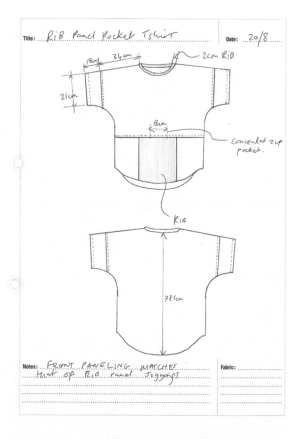

Title: Rib Panel Pocket Tshirt   Date: 20/8

2cm Rib

18cm   34cm

21cm

8cm

Concealed zip pocket.

Rib

78.5cm

Notes: FRONT PANELING MATCHES
Hint of Rib Panel Joggings

Fabric:

LINE BOARDS (COLLEGE AND INDUSTRY)

Flats may be presented on line boards to give an idea of range coordination, showing individual styles and colorways. Boards produced for industry (bottom), and used in presentations, are likely to be much more extensive and detailed than those produced in college (below), but the intention of both is to give an overall picture of a line or collection of styles.

Line boards, featuring working drawings and style colorways, may also be developed to illustrate delivery "packs" within a seasonal collection. A delivery pack is the specific combination of merchandise that will be delivered to stores at a particular point in the season, which may represent a key "look" that is relevant for that point in time.

The flat drawings from a line board can also be used by a catalog planner or merchandiser to visualize the line in different store classifications, allowing them to determine the size of the buy and to imagine how much of a line will work in store.

LINE SHEETS (INDUSTRY)

A line sheet is usually produced in industry, rather than in college, and includes miniature flats, often the same drawings as on the spec sheet, showing all the styles in a line. It is presented in tabular form with additional information, such as sales figures, order quantities, delivery period, and manufacturing and selling price. An assistant buyer or merchandiser may use this information to update critical paths and delivery dates.

LOOK BOOKS (INDUSTRY)

Look books and price lists may sometimes contain flats alongside a catwalk shot or illustration of a style to show the buyer an accurate interpretation of the garment.

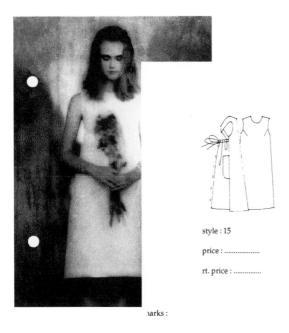

style : 15

price : ....

rt. price : ....

narks :

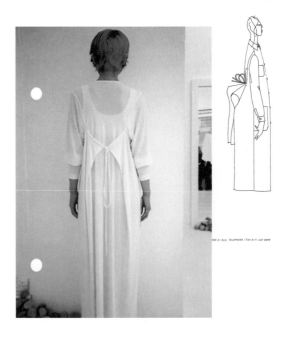

SIZE SPECIFICATION OR "SPEC" SHEETS (STUDY AND INDUSTRY)

A specification sheet, or "spec" includes a flat (including front and back views, and, if necessary, a side view and internal views), plus all the detailed measurements required to produce the garment (length, width, spacing, as well as indicators of stitch types, sewing operations, fabric, trims, hardware, and special treatments). Enlargements of small details may also be used to highlight important features. These details provide a list of "instructions." The sheets are used to ensure accurate fit.

The measurements are either added to the drawing itself, or else included in a table or size chart beside it. The pattern maker must be able to make the pattern using the information provided on the sheet, while the machinist, the maker, or the factory should be able to understand how the style should look in order to make up a sample. Accuracy is therefore vital. If a detail is omitted the sample will not be correct, and valuable time and money will have been wasted.

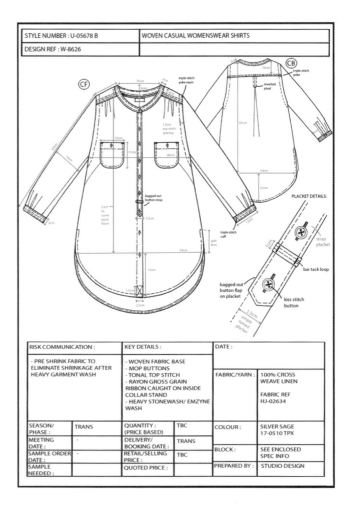

COSTING SHEETS (COLLEGE AND INDUSTRY)

A costing sheet lists all the elements needed to make up a garment (fabric, trims, cost of manufacture), which are then used to calculate the manufacturing, gross margin, and selling price of a style. Flats or photographs are sometimes added to costing sheets as a visual representation of the garment.

COSTING

Season: XXX		Style Number:	XXXXX	
		Style Name:	Wrap Dress	

Piece Goods	Description	Cost per Metre	Meterage Required	Cost
Fabric 1		11	3	33
Lining		3	2	6
Interfacing				
Other				
			Subtotal	39

Trimmings	Description	Unit Cost	No of Units	Cost
Buttons		1.2	5	1
Zippers		0.2	1	1.2
Threads				
Labels		0.2	2	0.4
Trims 1		2.5	3	7.5
Trims 2				
			Subtotal	10.1

Labour		Cost
First Sample	$50 divided across the 10 dresses produced	5
Pattern Cutting	$125 divided across the 10 dresses produced	12.5
Grading	$20 divided across the 10 dresses produced	2
CMT		25
	Subtotal	44.5

Shipping		Cost
Bags/Boxes		0.1
Hangers		
Swingtickets		0.2
Other		
	Subtotal	0.3

Total Cost of Goods Sold	93.9
Wholesale Markup	2.5
Wholesale Price	234.75
Retail Markup	2.7
Recommended Retail Price	633.825

TREND-PREDICTION WEBSITES (INDUSTRY)

Trend-prediction companies may use a particular type of
"enhanced" technical drawing—known as floats in the US—
to indicate key shapes and silhouettes. Artistic license is
often applied here.

Fashion Snoops is a subscription-based online trend-forecasting service that provides global trend insights to design professionals. Here is a typical web page showing predictions for women's outerwear, F/W 2016.

MERCHANDISING PLANS (INDUSTRY)

Visual merchandisers may use flats on merchandising plans to help to plan the display of garments prior to the collection arriving in store. The plan shown here uses 3D visual merchandising software to depict clothing within a store environment. Photographs of finished garments are often used, but here flats have been incorporated so that the layout can be planned right from the start of the design development process. The software even allows for the drawings to be "folded" for shelf display and fitted on to store dummies.

SEWING PATTERN CATALOGS AND PATTERN INSTRUCTIONS

Pattern books for domestic dressmaking usually include a full figure illustration accompanied by flats showing front and back views to clarify the style and indicate construction details for the customer. The paper pattern envelope and internal instruction sheet similarly include the flats, to facilitate construction.

The drawings are usually very basic, to ensure clarity and assist the dressmaker in construction. They are often supported by color drawings of all the pattern pieces, which may include grain lines and other technical details. Side views and enlarged sections (showing details) may also appear here.

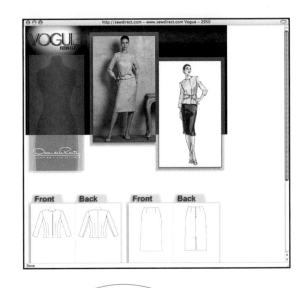

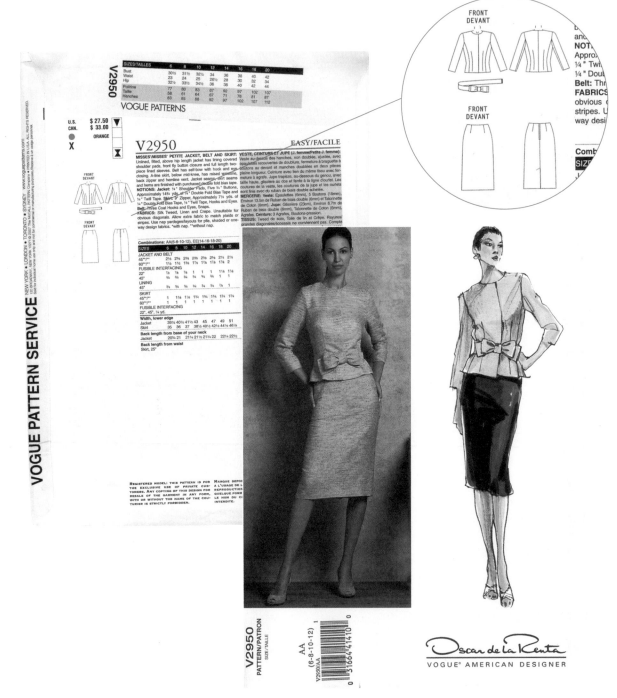

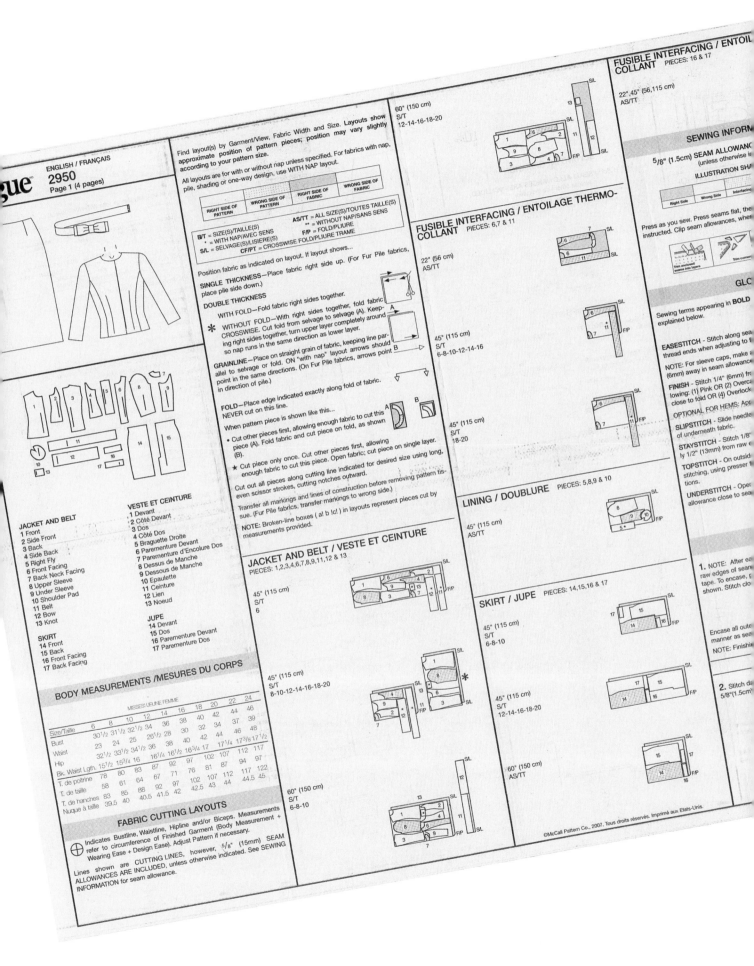

Find layout(s) by Garment/View, Fabric Width and Size. Layouts show approximate position of pattern pieces; position may vary slightly according to your pattern size.

All layouts are for with or without nap unless specified. For fabrics with nap, pile, shading or one-way design, use WITH NAP layout.

		RIGHT SIDE OF FABRIC	WRONG SIDE OF FABRIC
RIGHT SIDE OF PATTERN	WRONG SIDE OF PATTERN		

B/T = SIZE(S)/TAILLE(S)
* = WITH NAP/AVEC SENS
S/L = SELVAGE(S)/LISIERE(S)
CF/PT = CROSSWISE FOLD/PLIURE TRAME

AS/TT = ALL SIZE(S)/TOUTES TAILLE(S)
** = WITHOUT NAP/SANS SENS
F/P = FOLD/PLIURE

Position fabric as indicated on layout. If layout shows...

SINGLE THICKNESS—Place fabric right side up. (For Fur Pile fabrics, place pile side down.)

DOUBLE THICKNESS
  WITH FOLD—Fold fabric right sides together, fold fabric
★ WITHOUT FOLD—With right sides together, fold fabric CROSSWISE. Cut fold from selvage to selvage (A). Keeping right sides together, turn upper layer completely around so nap runs in the same direction as lower layer.

GRAINLINE—Place on straight grain of fabric, keeping line parallel to selvage or fold. ON "with nap" layout arrows should point in the same directions. (On Fur Pile fabrics, arrows point in direction of pile.)

FOLD—Place edge indicated exactly along fold of fabric. NEVER cut on this line.

When pattern piece is shown like this...
• Cut other pieces first, allowing enough fabric to cut this piece (A). Fold fabric and cut piece on fold, as shown (B).
★ Cut piece only once. Cut other pieces first, allowing enough fabric to cut this piece. Open fabric; cut piece on single layer.

Cut out all pieces along cutting line indicated for desired size using long, even scissor strokes, cutting notches outward.

Transfer all markings and lines of construction before removing pattern tissue. (Fur Pile fabrics, transfer markings to wrong side.)

NOTE: Broken-line boxes (a! b !c!) in layouts represent pieces cut by measurements provided.

JACKET AND BELT
1 Front
2 Side Front
3 Back
4 Side Back
5 Right Fly
6 Front Facing
7 Back Neck Facing
8 Upper Sleeve
9 Under Sleeve
10 Shoulder Pad
11 Belt
12 Bow
13 Knot

SKIRT
14 Front
15 Back
16 Front Facing
17 Back Facing

VESTE ET CEINTURE
1 Devant
2 Côté Devant
3 Dos
4 Côté Dos
5 Braguette Droite
6 Parementure Devant
7 Parementure d'Encolure Dos
8 Dessus de Manche
9 Dessous de Manche
10 Epaulette
11 Ceinture
12 Lien
13 Noeud

JUPE
14 Devant
15 Dos
16 Parementure Devant
17 Parementure Dos

BODY MEASUREMENTS / MESURES DU CORPS

				MISSES/JEUNE FEMME					
Size/Taille	6	8	10	12	14	16	18	20	22	24
Bust	30½	31½	32½	34	36	38	40	42	44	46
	23	24	25	26½	28	30	32	34	37	39
Waist	32½	33½	34½	36		40	42	44	46	48
Hip	15½	15¾	16	16¼	16½	16¾	17	17¼	17⅜	17½
Bk. Waist Lgth.							102	107	112	117
T. de poitrine	78	80	83	87	92	97				
T. de taille	58	61	64	67	71	76	81	87	94	97
T. de hanches	83	85	88	92		102	107	112	117	122
Nuque à taille	39.5	40	40.5	41.5	42	42.5	43	44	44.5	45

FABRIC CUTTING LAYOUTS

⊕ Indicates Bustline, Waistline, Hipline and/or Biceps. Measurements refer to circumference of Finished Garment (Body Measurement + Wearing Ease + Design Ease). Adjust Pattern if necessary.

Lines shown are CUTTING LINES, however, ⅝" (15mm) SEAM ALLOWANCES ARE INCLUDED, unless otherwise indicated. See SEWING INFORMATION for seam allowance.

FUSIBLE INTERFACING / ENTOILAGE THERMO-COLLANT PIECES: 6,7 & 11

22" (56 cm)
AS/TT

45" (115 cm)
S/T
6-8-10-12-14-16

45" (115 cm)
S/T
18-20

LINING / DOUBLURE PIECES: 5,8,9 & 10

45" (115 cm)
AS/TT

SKIRT / JUPE PIECES: 14,15,16 & 17

45" (115 cm)
S/T
6-8-10

45" (115 cm)
S/T
12-14-16-18-20

60" (150 cm)
AS/TT

JACKET AND BELT / VESTE ET CEINTURE PIECES: 1,2,3,4,6,7,8,9,11,12 & 13

45" (115 cm)
S/T
6

45" (115 cm)
S/T
8-10-12-14-16-18-20

60" (150 cm)
S/T
6-8-10

60" (150 cm)
S/T
12-14-16-18-20

FUSIBLE INTERFACING / ENTOILAGE COLLANT PIECES: 16 & 17

22", 45" (56,115 cm)
AS/TT

SEWING INFORMATION

⅝" (1.5cm) SEAM ALLOWANCE
(unless otherwise in

ILLUSTRATION SHA

Right Side	Wrong Side	Interfacing

Press as you sew. Press seams flat, the instructed. Clip seam allowances, whe

GLOSSARY

Sewing terms appearing in BOLD explained below.

EASESTITCH - Stitch along se thread ends when adjusting to fit.

NOTE: For sleeve caps, make e (6mm) away in seam allowance

FINISH - Stitch 1/4" (6mm) from lowing: (1) Pink OR (2) Overcas close to fold OR (4) Overlock

OPTIONAL FOR HEMS: App

SLIPSTITCH - Slide needle of underneath fabric.

STAYSTITCH - Stitch 1/8 ly 1/2" (13mm) from raw e

TOPSTITCH - On outside stitching, using presser f tions.

UNDERSTITCH - Open allowance close to seam

1. NOTE: After ea raw edges of sea tape. To encase, p shown. Stitch

Encase all oute manner as sea

NOTE: Finishi

2. Stitch da
⅝"(1.5cm

©McCall Pattern Co., 2007. Tous droits réservés. Imprimé aux Etats-Unis.

How to create flats

The process of producing flats, demonstrated here, begins with the creation of a generic body form. This is a basic body shape that can be used as a template and starting point for every flat that you make. The next step involves drawing the garment style. Once you have created a garment style, you can either go on to create the finished flat, or use it as inspiration for drawing a range of styles before selecting those that you wish to develop into final flats. This technique of developing designs through flat drawing is called speed designing (see page 31).

CREATING A GENERIC TEMPLATE

As the first stage in the process of technical drawing it is worth taking some time to draw an accurate generic template, or body shape. Once you have perfected this outline, it may be used as a foundation to produce all your flats. For the purposes of technical drawing, to create a more visually appealing silhouette, the body is elongated and streamlined through the lower and central sections. It is also useful to draw a side view (far right, opposite page) as some garments may benefit from being drawn from this angle.

You can draw your outline by hand or using CAD, or using a combination of the two. Since this outline will be used many times, it is worth keeping a master outline in your portfolio for future use or reference. You may find, when working in industry, that you will have different templates for different clients, lines, and markets, depending on their preference. It is important that you bear this in mind when producing work for specific markets.

AVERAGE FEMALE FIGURE

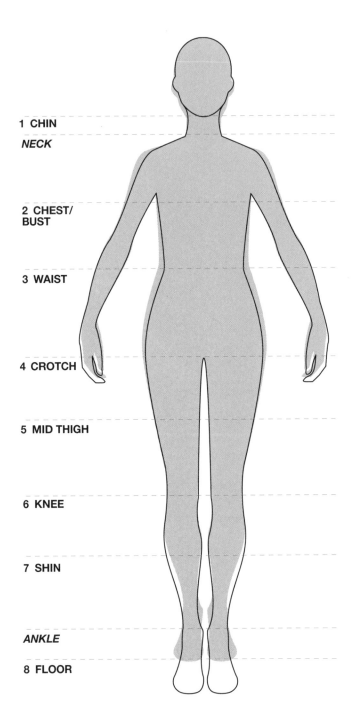

1 CHIN

NECK

2 CHEST/BUST

3 WAIST

4 CROTCH

5 MID THIGH

6 KNEE

7 SHIN

ANKLE

8 FLOOR

USING A GENERIC TEMPLATE

It is important to understand that one generic template will not be suitable for use at all levels of the industry or in different parts of the world. Body shapes vary from market to market, as well as between different cultures. A female template aimed at the UK or US market might look overweight and too curvaceous to a Far East customer, for example, where the female body shape is different. Garment drawings should reflect the desired market accurately and, therefore, the template needs to be adjusted accordingly each time a different market is attempted. Below is a generic "western" template.

GENERIC TEMPLATE

Front view   Side view

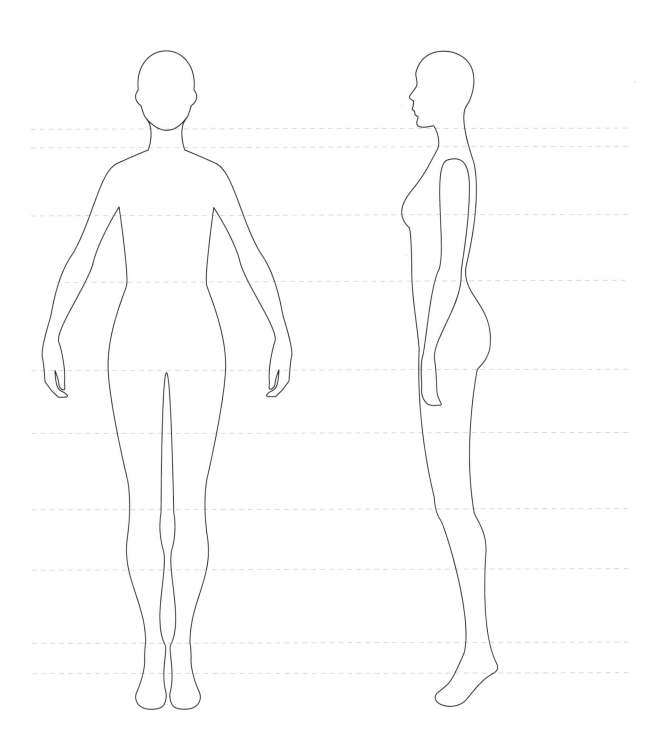

DIFFERENT BODY POSITIONS

It is useful to work with a template with different arm and leg positions, particularly when working on garments where these areas need to be clearly defined, or when developing wider styles.

GENERIC TEMPLATE

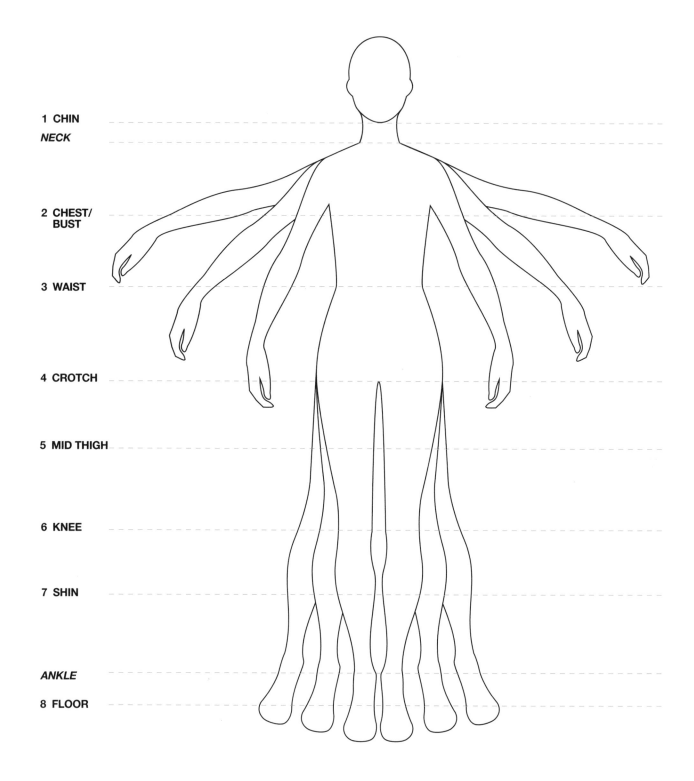

1 CHIN

NECK

2 CHEST/
  BUST

3 WAIST

4 CROTCH

5 MID THIGH

6 KNEE

7 SHIN

ANKLE

8 FLOOR

GENERIC TEMPLATE

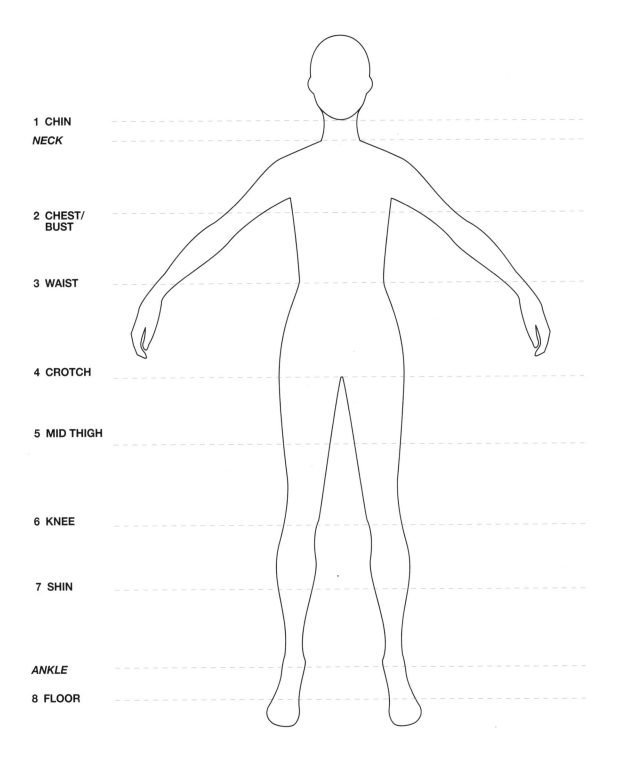

1 CHIN

NECK

2 CHEST/
  BUST

3 WAIST

4 CROTCH

5 MID THIGH

6 KNEE

7 SHIN

ANKLE

8 FLOOR

GENERIC TEMPLATE

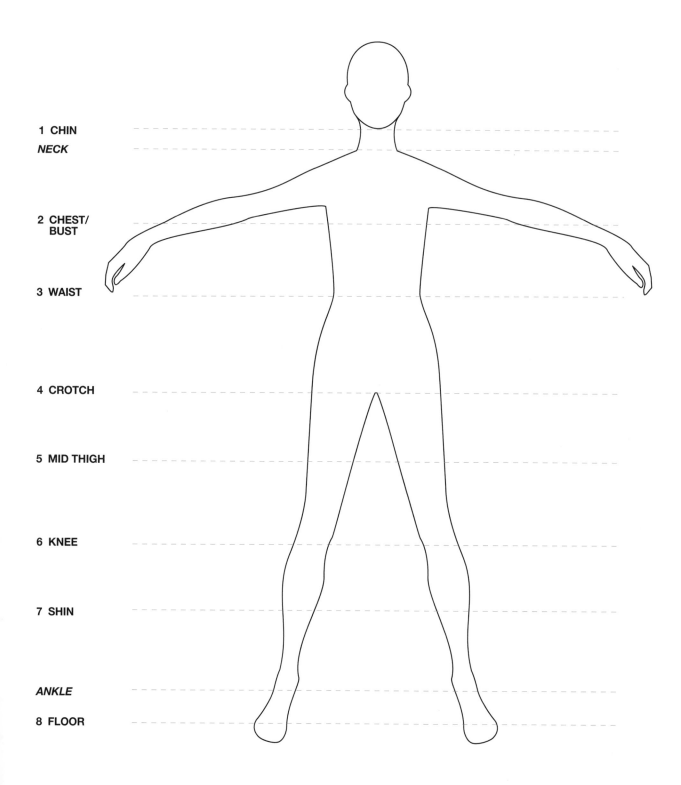

1 CHIN

NECK

2 CHEST/ BUST

3 WAIST

4 CROTCH

5 MID THIGH

6 KNEE

7 SHIN

ANKLE

8 FLOOR

ADAPTING FOR DIFFERENT MARKETS

The figure, below left, shows how the generic template may be adapted into a teenage template, and below right shows a plus size. The teenage template may also be used for other markets, such as the Asian market, where smaller body frames are indigenous. Knowledge of the differences in markets and body shapes is necessary in order to create commercially and aesthetically pleasing templates. If you are designing for a "plus size" market, you would not use your generic template as it is clearly too narrow. The final drawings should reflect the required outcome as much as possible.

TEEN TEMPLATE

+ SIZE TEMPLATE

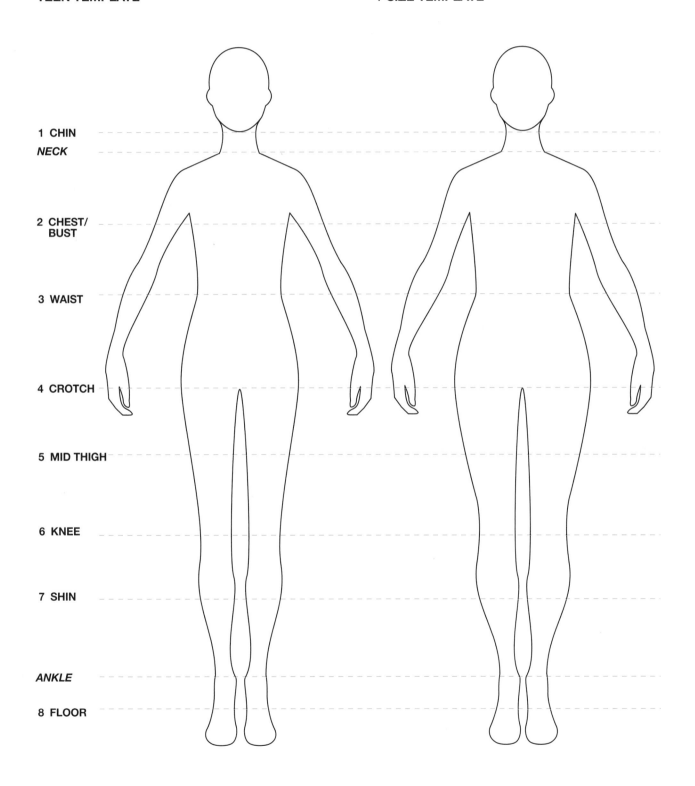

1 CHIN

NECK

2 CHEST/ BUST

3 WAIST

4 CROTCH

5 MID THIGH

6 KNEE

7 SHIN

ANKLE

8 FLOOR

Drawing from a garment

Flats can also be developed from an existing garment. If you are speed designing, you may also be drawing from an existing garment, using it as inspiration or using its basic silhouette as the foundation for your own designs. Using garments from your wardrobe is also the best way to practice your drawing technique, especially if you are unsure where to position styling details.

Begin by laying out the garment on the floor. You should always draw from a "plan view," from a head-on perspective, so you will need to stand directly above the garment. You may need to stand on a chair to view it correctly. Lay the garment down naturally. If you force it into an unnatural position your drawing will be distorted.

Sometimes a back view of part of a garment is required, such as the back of a sleeve. Working with your garment laid flat allows you to manipulate it in ways that would not be possible were it on a hanger.

Do not view the garment from an angle as your drawing will be distorted by perspective. This may occur if you lay the garment on a table and sit on a chair in front of it—you will not be able to see the silhouette properly.

Hanging the garment on a hanger will introduce the effects of gravity, which will also cause distortion. Garments do not "hang" symmetrically.

Technical drawing by hand using the generic template

Once you have laid out your garment correctly, you are ready to start drawing. This step-by-step sequence shows how to make variations of a flared skirt using the technique of speed designing, and subsequently demonstrates how to complete the flats.

MATERIALS REQUIRED
Tracing paper

Layout paper (45 gsm) or any semi-opaque paper that you can still see through over a light box

Sheets of white paper, Letter or Legal sized

Low-tack adhesive tape to secure your tracing paper over templates

Mechanical pencil with HB leads (0.5mm) (Do not use pencils any softer than HB, or the line will not be fine enough)

Black fine-liner pens:
• 0.01mm for ultra-fine stitch detail
• 0.1mm for stitch and seam detail
• 0.3mm for all main lines except stitch detail
• 0.6mm/0.8mm for outline definition if needed for line boards or presentation purposes (fine-line fiber-tip pens tend to give a sharper line than nylon-tip pens)

15cm flat **rule**
30cm flat **rule** (with right angle and parallel guides) or a set square

French curve

Scissors

Scalpel or craft knife with blades

GENERIC TEMPLATE

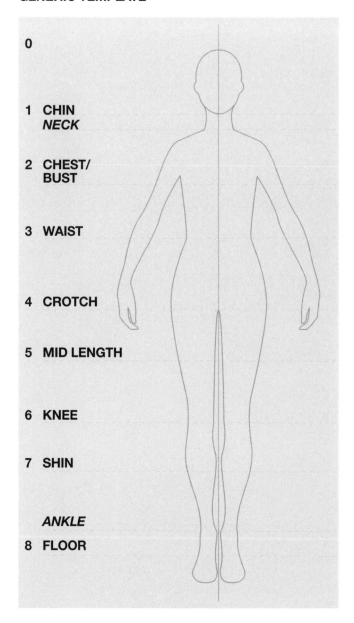

0

1 CHIN
   NECK

2 CHEST/
   BUST

3 WAIST

4 CROTCH

5 MID LENGTH

6 KNEE

7 SHIN

   ANKLE

8 FLOOR

STEP 1
Place your template beneath a letter-size piece of tracing paper. Adhere the tracing paper to the template with low-tack tape. With a pencil and using a long rule, draw a vertical line through the center of the template, and right down the page. You will now draw the left- or right-hand side of the garment only, depending on what feels more natural to you. Draw on one side only. When working, remember that you are only drawing half the garment.

GENERIC TEMPLATE

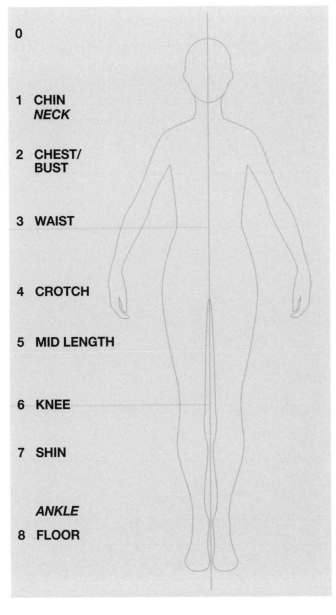

0

1 **CHIN**
NECK

2 **CHEST/ BUST**

3 **WAIST**

4 **CROTCH**

5 **MID LENGTH**

6 **KNEE**

7 **SHIN**

ANKLE

8 **FLOOR**

GENERIC TEMPLATE

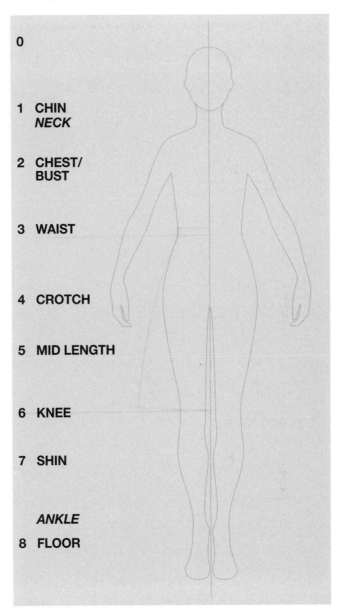

0

1 **CHIN**
NECK

2 **CHEST/ BUST**

3 **WAIST**

4 **CROTCH**

5 **MID LENGTH**

6 **KNEE**

7 **SHIN**

ANKLE

8 **FLOOR**

STEP 2

Using your set square, mark the waistline at right angles to the center line. Mark the position of the kneeline with a set square too. These markers will help you make sure your drawing is in proportion later.

STEP 3

Draw a skirt style on one side of the template. Rotating the paper sometimes makes it easier to "disconnect" yourself from the idea that you are drawing a garment and allows you to focus on creating smooth and accurate lines. Use a rule if necessary when straight lines are required, and draw freehand or use a French curve to achieve smooth curves. A rule with right-angle guidelines will be useful to ensure accuracy.

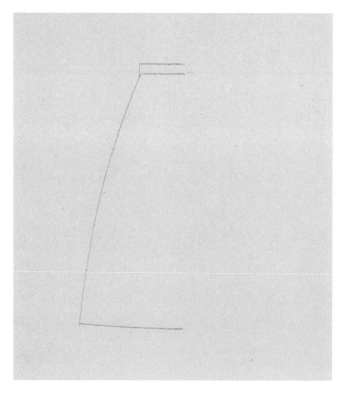

STEP 4

When you have completed your style, remove the template. Fold the tracing paper in half along the vertical center line, with the side on which you have drawn the half of the skirt on the outside. Make sure you fold the tracing paper as accurately as possible on the center line when tracing through, or you will find that the final drawing is not symmetrical and you will have to start again.

STEP 5

With a white sheet of paper beneath (to enable you to see what you are drawing), trace the lines of the flared skirt through to the other side of the center line. Be careful when working with pencil on tracing paper, as lines may smudge. This is why you should use an HB or harder lead.

STEP 6

Open out the tracing paper and tidy up your drawing, going over any faint lines. Make sure that any lines crossing the center-front vertical line are smooth and at right angles. Consider how one would get in and out of the garment; add in openings and fastenings. At this stage you can either complete your flat (follow the written instructions in Steps 9–11) or use the technique of speed designing to continue to make variations of the style.

SPEED DESIGNING

Speed designing omits the sketch phase of design work and is particularly useful if you are working on uncomplicated, more commercial design ideas, especially if given specific guidelines by a client who, for example, might commission a line of casual skirts or jackets. Once a garment style has been drawn using the generic template, that style can then be used as a template for developing variations of that garment. Working with your knowledge of construction and pattern cutting, you will be able to draw real working garments, rather than just sketching out rough ideas. Every line you draw will be valid and in the correct position.

All the design development is worked in pencil on tracing paper to create a series of roughs. Each design may inspire another variation; sometimes a simple alteration to a drawing, such as a change in skirt length, waist height, or pants width, will produce a completely new alternative. Small differences between styles will provide more options for selection. Variations can be produced at great speed, accelerated by drawing only half the garment. Each rough may take as little as a couple of minutes to draw, allowing numerous design solutions to be explored.

By working from the generic template, all subsequent styles will be in proportion to each other; an advantage if they are all finally to be positioned together on one page, such as on a line plan. The advantage of working in this way over sketching is speed, allied to drawings that are "real" clothes. Once you have mastered the basic principles of speed designing, you will be able to develop your own unique way of applying the process to suit your needs.

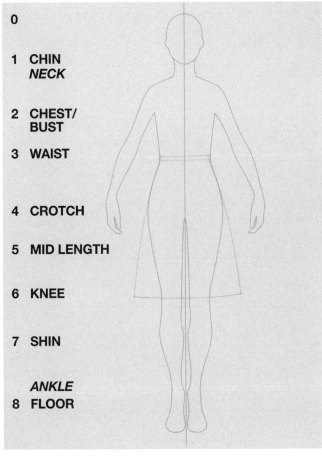

0

1 CHIN
NECK

2 CHEST/
BUST

3 WAIST

4 CROTCH

5 MID LENGTH

6 KNEE

7 SHIN

ANKLE
8 FLOOR

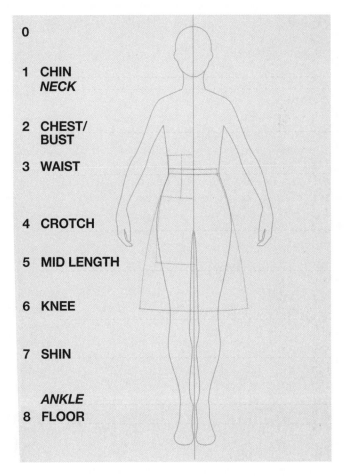

0

1 CHIN
NECK

2 CHEST/
BUST

3 WAIST

4 CROTCH

5 MID LENGTH

6 KNEE

7 SHIN

ANKLE
8 FLOOR

STEP 7

Using the speed designing technique, here we will use this drawing to create another skirt, this time a knee-length style with a high waist. Place the original traced drawing over the template again, then place a new sheet of tracing paper on top. Draw the center-front line. Make sure all three sheets are secured with low-tack tape.

STEP 8

You can continue to create styles using your original drawing, one style developing into another. There are endless possibilities, and just by changing the length or seam details you can create a new design. In this drawing there are four possible style options: two high waists (different lengths) and two dropped waists (flared and straight).

Once you have a style you want to develop, you may work on a full drawing (not just one side), particularly if the style is complex or asymmetric.

STEP 9

To complete your flat, select one of your designs. You can complete the process by hand or scan the drawing and complete it using CAD. To complete by hand, place your tracing beneath a piece of layout paper and secure it with low-tack tape. You can also work on a light box at this stage, if you have one available, or on a window. You may need to darken the lines of your tracing in order to see it through the layout paper. Test the paper, making sure your pen doesn't "bleed" on it. Trace over the lines of your design using a 0.3mm fine-line fiber-tip pen.

STEP 10

Use a 0.01mm fine-line fiber-tip pen to draw in stitches or any fine detailing. If you have a very detailed garment, enlarge your original pencil drawing on a photocopier and draw as large as is comfortable. When the drawing is complete, reduce back down to the required proportions. Remember to note the percentage increase so that you can reduce the drawing back down accurately, otherwise this drawing will be disproportionate to others if featured in a group or on a line board.

STEP 11

For a particular effect, or if desired, using a 0.8mm fine-line fiber-tip pen, draw a heavy black line around the outside of your drawing (this would not be used on a spec or costing sheet, only if the drawing is to be used for presentation purposes).

Your technical drawing is now ready to photocopy, scan, or use as you wish.

Back views

Once you have completed the front view of a garment, you can use it to develop the back view. The external silhouette will be almost identical to that of the front view. Here we will continue with an example of a skirt. Follow the exercise below to see how first one style morphs into another, then how a back view is easily created from a front.

STEP 1

Using a rule, draw a center line on a piece of tracing paper. Working from the last straight, high-waisted style, develop a low-waisted A-line skirt in pencil, working in half on tracing paper. Draw lines for both the front and back view at the same time.

STEP 2

Trace off half the silhouette along this center line. Once you have the entire back view, check for symmetry and make any adjustments.

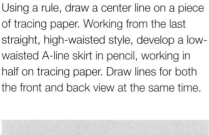

STEP 3

You may find it useful to use a colored pencil at this stage so that you can clearly see the lines you are drawing over the template. When working out a back view, make sure any seams from the front joining the side are followed through from the exact same point, unless different. Don't forget to include openings.

DOS & DON'TS

1   If you are drawing a very detailed garment, you may wish to work on legal-size paper so that you can more easily draw complex details and reduce the size later with the aid of a scanner or photocopier.

2   Never use softer than an HB lead, or your drawing line will not be fine enough for accuracy, and it will smudge.

3   Be prepared to redraw until your rough drawing is how you want it.

4   Always use low-tack adhesive tape to secure tracings to stop the paper moving around.

5   Rotate your drawing throughout the process: it is easier to draw smooth lines when a line is vertical rather than horizontal.

6   Always make sure a line crossing the center front or center back is at a right angle, for symmetry.

7   Use a rule where necessary for straight lines, but blend through at a curve to soften. Never draw a curve with a rule, use a French curve!

8   Never use a fine-line pen on tracing paper as it will not dry and will smudge: only use it on layout paper.

9   Wash hands regularly when working on tracings to avoid smudges when you transfer to layout.

10 Work in good overhead light so that you can see through the layout paper, or ideally work on a light box.

11 You may have to start a final pen drawing a few times because of wobbly lines: have patience.

12 Always try to work with a sheet of white paper under your work as it will absorb any excess lead when tracing as well as show up a tracing under layout paper better when you are producing a final pen drawing.

13 When working on your final pen drawing, clean the edge of the rule as often as possible, as the edge collects ink and this may transfer to your drawing.

14 Use a variety of fine-line pens (0.05mm and 0.1–0.3mm) to add depth to your final drawing.

Technical drawing from the generic template using Illustrator

This step-by-step sequence shows how to create a flat of a shirt using Illustrator, how to add color and pattern, and how to develop variations with speed designing.

CREATING THE BODICE

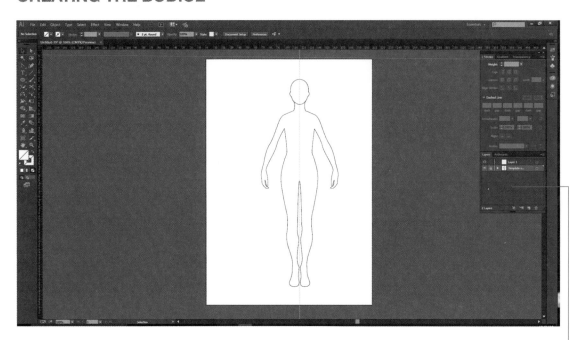

STEP 1

Start by opening your template. If you are using the .ai file, open your template and lock the template layer, then create a new layer to begin the shirt on. You can also place your template by opening a new file first, **File > New**.

With your new file open, go to **File > Place**. Find your template, select the Template button, and ensure that Link is not checked. Check Place. This will automatically create two different layers—a Template layer that will be locked and dimmed, and a new layer, called Layer 1, where you can begin creating your shirt.

Unlock your Template layer for the moment and go to **View > Rulers > Show Rulers**. From the vertical rule panel, drag the rule and place it in the center of your template. Lock the layer again—it's very important that your template and rule don't move during the process. You can also lock the rule by right clicking and selecting the Lock Guides option.

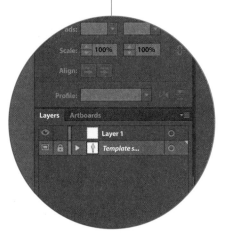

Create two layers. The Template layer should mostly be kept locked throughout.

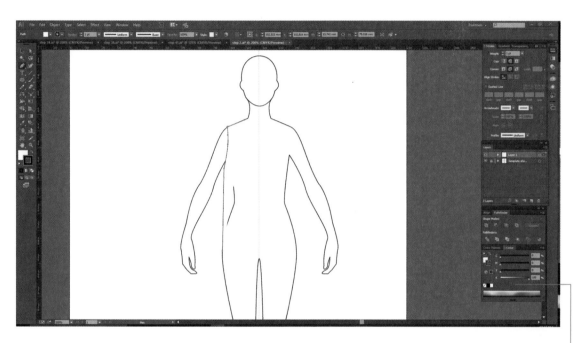

STEP 2

Make sure you are on Layer 1. Use the Zoom tool to zoom in on the area you will be working on, or the keyboard shortcut Ctrl/Cmd+ or Ctrl/Cmd- to zoom in and out. Select the Pen tool and make sure you have the black line and white fill in your graphic status. Click on Stroke in the toolbar and select 1-pt weight Uniform stroke. Go to **Window > Stroke** to bring up the Stroke menu and select round edges in Corner and Cap.

With the Pen tool first click on the high point shoulder, then click on the low point shoulder. The next click should be inside the armhole, then click under the armhole. Your final click should be at the hip. Use the Direct Selection tool if you need to correct the placement of your anchors and use the Anchor Point tool to create a smooth armhole. Make sure you're dragging outward when using the Anchor Point tool, to avoid tangling. You have created half of your bodice.

In the Pen tool menu select the white fill and black line.

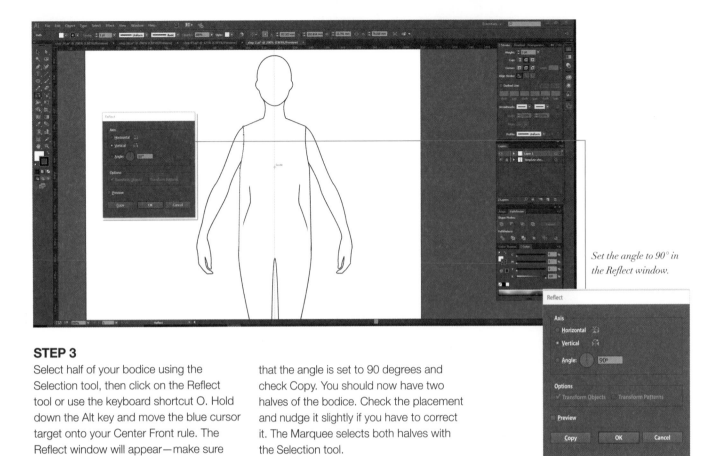

Set the angle to 90° in the Reflect window.

STEP 3

Select half of your bodice using the Selection tool, then click on the Reflect tool or use the keyboard shortcut O. Hold down the Alt key and move the blue cursor target onto your Center Front rule. The Reflect window will appear—make sure that the angle is set to 90 degrees and check Copy. You should now have two halves of the bodice. Check the placement and nudge it slightly if you have to correct it. The Marquee selects both halves with the Selection tool.

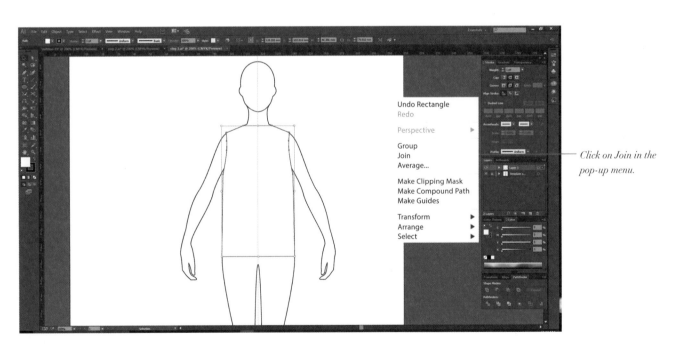

Click on Join in the pop-up menu.

STEP 4

With both halves selected using the Selection tool, right click (PC) or Ctrl click (Mac) to bring up a pop-up menu: click on Join. The upper part of your bodice has now joined. Click on Join a second time for the lower part of your shirt to join. You now have the whole bodice.

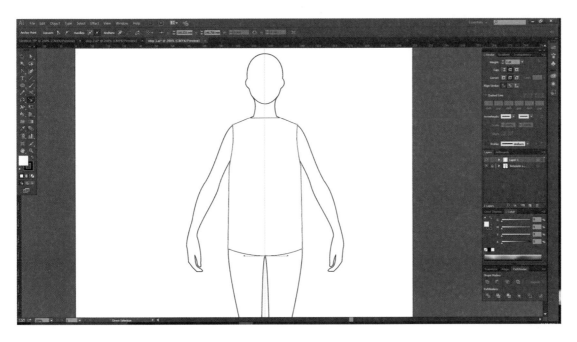

STEP 5

Gently curve the hemline of your shirt. With the Direct Selection tool, click anywhere outside your shape. Now select the whole shape of your bodice with the same Direct Selection tool. This will allow you to use the Reshape tool from the toolbox menu. It's located next to the Reflect tool. Pick up the hemline and drag down with the Reshape tool, curving the hemline. The Reshape tool will add an anchor point in the middle. If necessary, go back to the Anchor Point tool to adjust the curve by dragging the arrows on both sides. Make sure you don't twist and drag the arrows outward. If the curve twists, untwist and start again until you are happy with it. You can do the same for the neckline if you wish. You don't need a curved neckline here—you are going to create a shirt collar, which will sit on top.

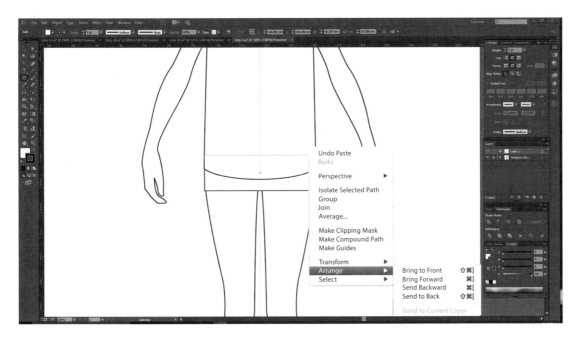

STEP 6

You are now going to create the back part of the shirt that is visible from the front. Use the Rectangle tool but hold the Alt key so the rectangle shape will start from the center. Start from the Center Front line and create the rectangle shape. Make sure it has a white fill. Right click/Ctrl click; select Arrange and Send to Back and the new shape will appear behind the bodice. Adjust the anchor points if necessary— front and back should be perfectly aligned.

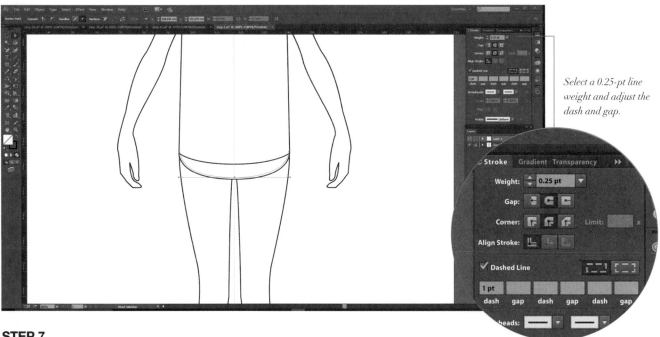

Select a 0.25-pt line weight and adjust the dash and gap.

STEP 7

Use the Direct Selection tool and click outside your rectangular shape, then click on the shape again. Use the Reshape tool to curve the hemline of the shirt back, just the same as with the front. Use the Delete Anchor tool or simply select using the white arrow to delete the corners of the rectangle. Adjust the shape with the

Anchor Point tool. When happy with the shape of the back, click on the middle anchor of your hem. Copy and paste in front (Ctrl/Cmd C and Ctrl/Cmd F). Nudge the line slightly; you will use this line to create the stitching. In your Stroke panel select a line weight of 0.25-pt and check Dashed Line. Adjust the dash and gap

as you would like—I've used a 1-pt dash here. Now you have the stitching. Make sure the stitching line has no fill, group with the back of the shirt, and bring the stitching to the front.

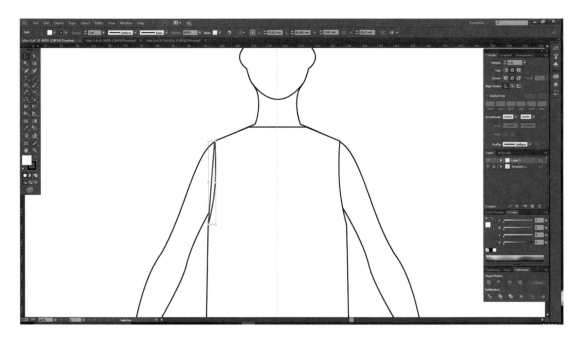

CREATING THE SLEEVES

STEP 1

Click on the anchor point in the middle of your armhole with the Direct Selection tool. Make sure both arrows are visible and the whole line is selected. Click Ctrl/Cmd C to copy the line and Ctrl/Cmd F to paste

the new line in front. You are now going to create a sleeve shape by right clicking/Ctrl clicking your mouse and selecting Join, just like when you were joining the bodice.

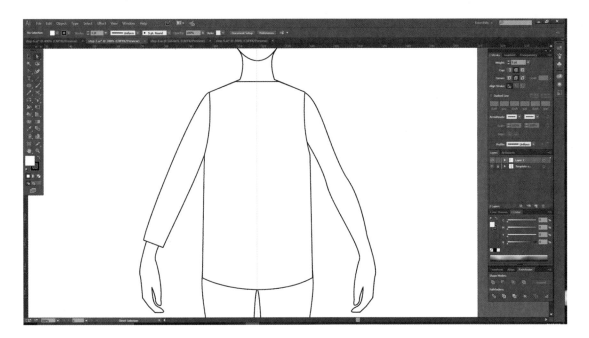

STEP 2

Select the Add Anchor Point tool and add two points anywhere on the joined line segment, one close to the top, one close to the bottom. Placing additional anchor points is not critical, as long as you do add two. Using the Direct Selection tool, click on a new anchor point and drag to create the sleeve. Do this with both points; you will be adding cuffs to the shirt, so the sleeve length should allow for this. Use the Anchor Point tool to adjust the shape of your sleeve.

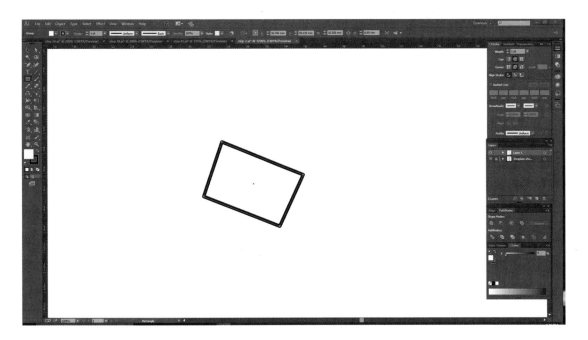

STEP 3

Create the cuff using the Rectangle tool. With the Direct Selection tool nudge the points on the bottom segment of your cuff. Use the Rotate tool to rotate your cuff and adjust the angle in relation to your sleeve.

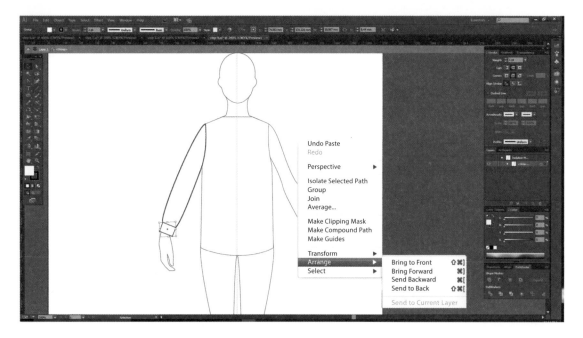

STEP 4

Select the cuff and sleeve, right click/Ctrl click and Group. Make sure the white fill is selected for both the cuff and the sleeve. To adjust the position of the cuff and sleeve you can use **Arrange > Bring to Front** to bring the cuff forward.

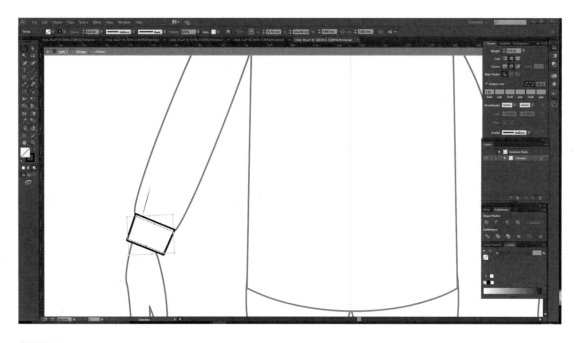

STEP 5

You will now add the stitching to the cuff by selecting the upper line of your cuff using the Direct Selection tool. Copy and paste in front. Nudge the copied line a couple of points down. Go to the Stroke menu and select a line weight of 0.25-pt. Check on the dashed line to create the stitching, and adjust so it's parallel. Repeat the process for the lower line of your cuff to create the stitching on the bottom. Make sure that the white fill is switched to No Fill on your stitching lines. You can now add the lines on your sleeve that will indicate the drape. Group the stitching and the drape line and Bring to Front, so you won't lose either of them when applying color. Now the whole sleeve is finished.

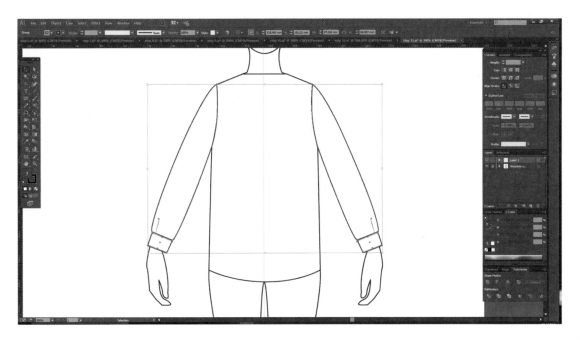

STEP 6

Reflect the sleeve using the same method used for the bodice. Click the O key on your keyboard to access the Reflect tool. Hold down the Alt key and place the cursor on the Center Front line. Check

Copy to duplicate the sleeve. Adjust if necessary and Group both of your sleeves.

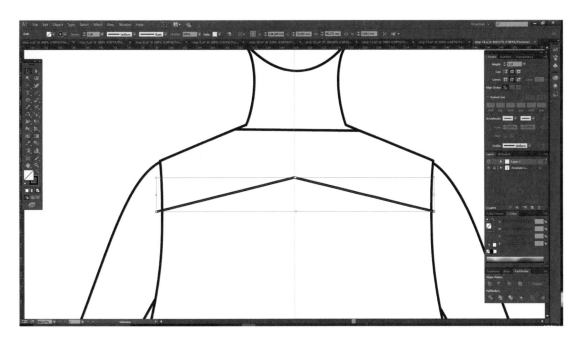

CREATING THE YOKE

STEP 1

To create the yoke, use the Pen tool to draw the line from outside the bodice shape, where your yoke placement should be, to the Center Front line. Finish the line on the other side. Illustrator will let you know when your lines are perfectly aligned. Alternatively, you can draw just half of the line up to the Center Front and then Reflect. If doing this, make sure you join both lines into a single line—you can use the Join tool to do this. The Join tool is located just above the Reflect tool; you can access it through the drop-down menu. For the separate yoke to be created, it's vital that your lines start and end outside the bodice shape. Make sure your yoke line has no fill.

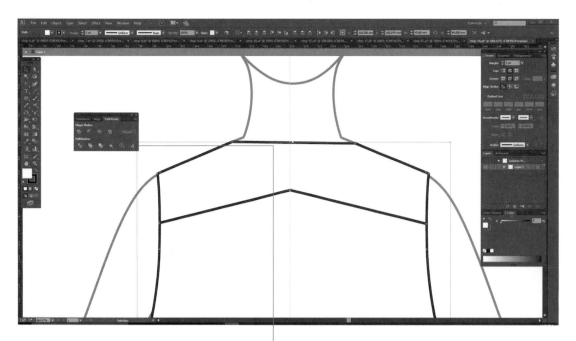

STEP 2

Direct Select the bodice. Hold down the Shift key to select the yoke line as well. Go to **Window > Pathfinder**. In the Pathfinder menu select Divide. When the shapes divide, click Ungroup to separate the yoke from the rest of the bodice.

Select Divide, the bottom left icon in the Pathfinder menu.

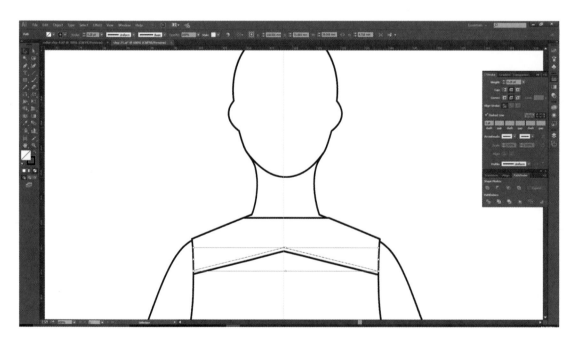

STEP 3

Create the stitching for the yoke, armholes and the hem of the bodice. Using the same method outlined in Step 7 of Creating the Bodice, create the stitching above the yoke and on the hem of your bodice. Group the yoke stitching with the yoke and Bring to Front by right clicking/ Ctrl clicking with your mouse to access the Arrange menu. Do the same for all the stitching on the bodice. Group all parts of your bodice.

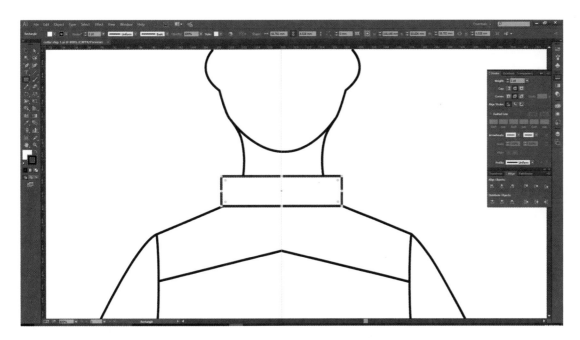

CREATING THE COLLAR

STEP 1

Using the Rectangle tool and holding down the Alt key so it draws from the center, place the cursor on the Center Front line. Create the shape, click to copy but don't paste it anywhere yet. You will use it later—this is going to be your collar stand.

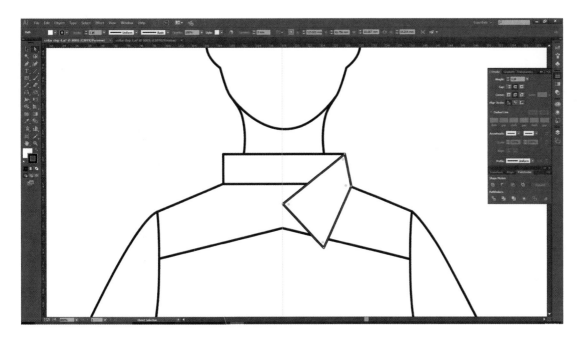

STEP 2

Starting from the Center Front, draw the shape of the collar with the Pen tool. First click on the Center Front, then under the yoke, then where the collar meets the shoulder. Your fourth click should close the shape on the collar stand. Make sure that the shape has a white fill.

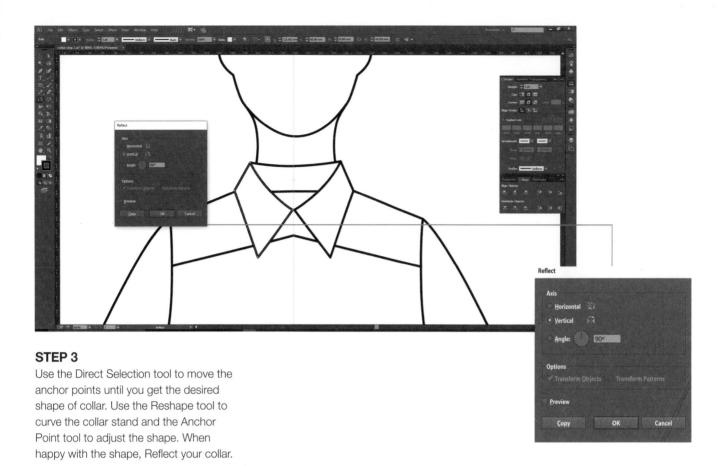

STEP 3

Use the Direct Selection tool to move the
anchor points until you get the desired
shape of collar. Use the Reshape tool to
curve the collar stand and the Anchor
Point tool to adjust the shape. When
happy with the shape, Reflect your collar.

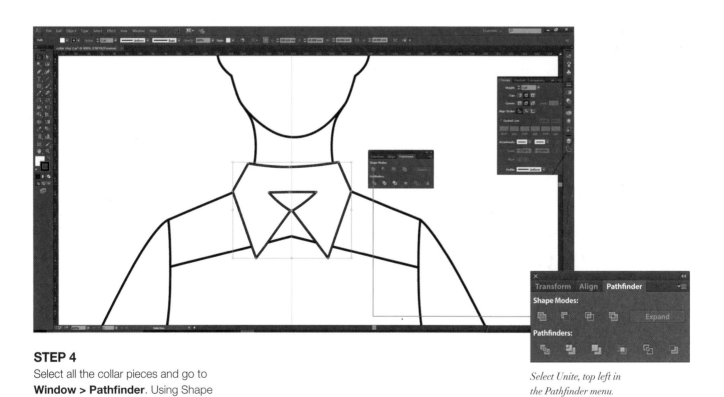

STEP 4

Select all the collar pieces and go to
Window > Pathfinder. Using Shape
Modes select the Unite option. You should
end up with something like this.

Select Unite, top left in
the Pathfinder menu.

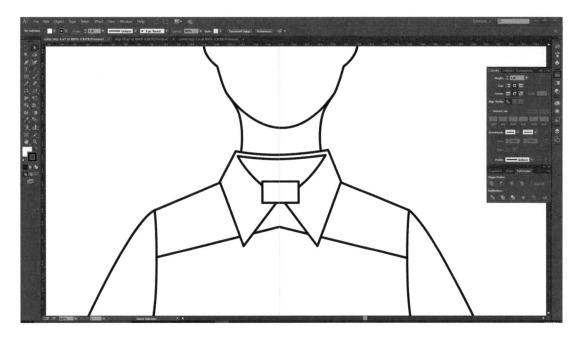

STEP 5

Using the Direct Selection tool, select the corner of the inside triangle and tuck it underneath the collar stand anchor point. Do the same for the other side. The collar will look like it's folded at the back of the neck. That is your collar roll. Now click on Ctrl/Cmd V to bring back the original rectangle shape of the collar that you created in Step 1 and copied for later. Send the shape back behind the collar. This is the back of the collar. Using the Rectangle tool again, create a new shape to fill in the missing gap and send this backward too.

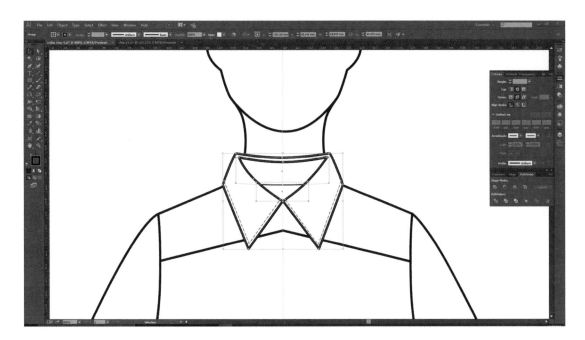

STEP 6

Proceed to create the stitching using the same method explained previously and then group the collar elements. The collar is now complete.

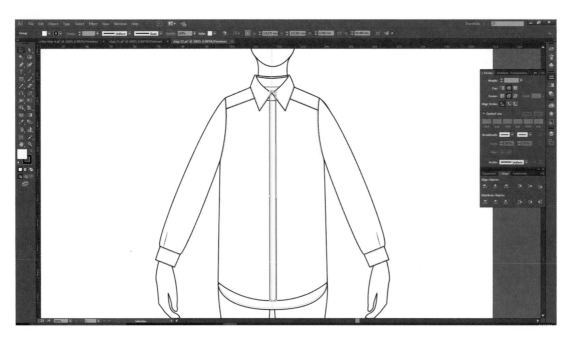

CREATING THE PLACKET

STEP 1

Using the Rectangle tool, create the placket and position it at the center of your shirt. Create the stitching on both sides and Bring to Front. Create the line at the top of the placket, under the collar. Make sure all placket elements are grouped and Send to Back, so it appears behind your collar. You can further center the placket by using the Align tab in the Pathfinder menu. Make sure you select both objects but go back and click on the bodice so the thick line appears around it. That's how you tell Illustrator to align the placket to your key object—the bodice. Use the Horizontal Align Center option.

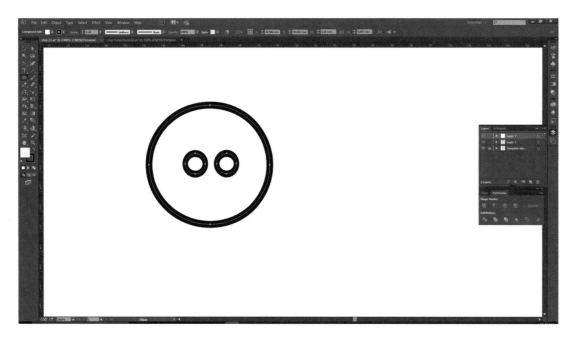

STEP 2

Using the Ellipse tool and holding the Alt key so you draw from the center, create a circle shape. This will be your button. Create a smaller circle and copy it. Position both small circles as buttonholes. Select All and go to **Window > Pathfinder**. In the Shape Modes, select Exclude (top right in the Pathfinder menu). Now you have the perfect fillable button.

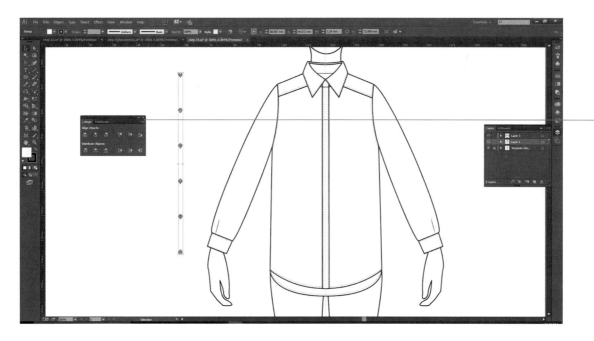

STEP 3

Use the Pen tool to add the thread to your button and finish with the button opening. Group all the button components and copy the button five times so that you end up with six buttons. You can copy the buttons by holding down the Alt key and dragging. Marquee select all the buttons and Align Horizontal Center. Put the buttons in a placket and align the buttons to the placket. Position the first and the last button correctly and use Distribute Objects from the Pathfinder menu. Click on Distribute Center for the buttons to redistribute accordingly.

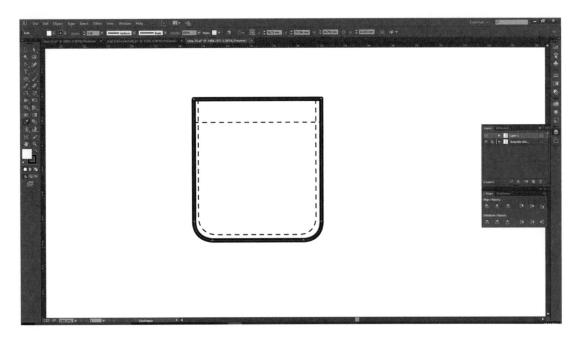

CREATING THE POCKET

STEP 1

Starting with the Rectangle tool, create the pocket. You can use a combination of Add Anchor Point, Delete Anchor Point, and the Anchor Point tools to perfect the shape of the pocket. Next, create the lines that will form the stitching, as explained previously. Direct Select a line that is intended as stitching, go to the Stroke menu and change the line to Dashed; select the Eyedropper tool from the toolbox and click on any of the existing stitching lines. The Eyedropper tool will perfectly replicate the existing stitching and convert your selected line into a stitch.

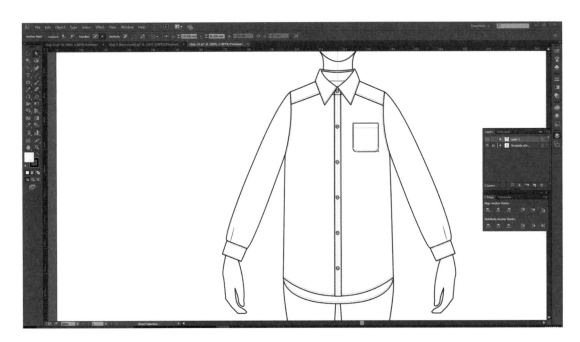

STEP 2

Place the pocket on your shirt. Your shirt is now complete.

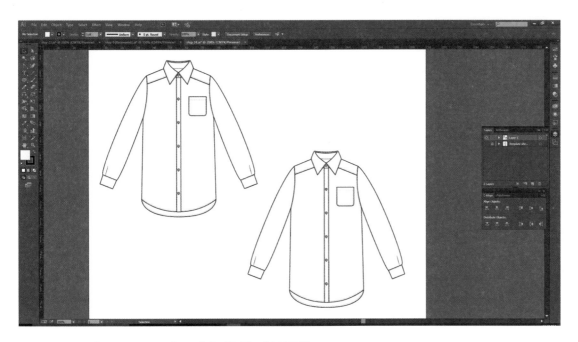

CREATING THE BACK OF THE SHIRT

STEP 1

Make sure your shirt is grouped before you copy it by holding down the Alt key. You can also switch the visibility off, so your template is not in the way. You won't need the template for this part because you will be using the front of the shirt to create the back of the shirt.

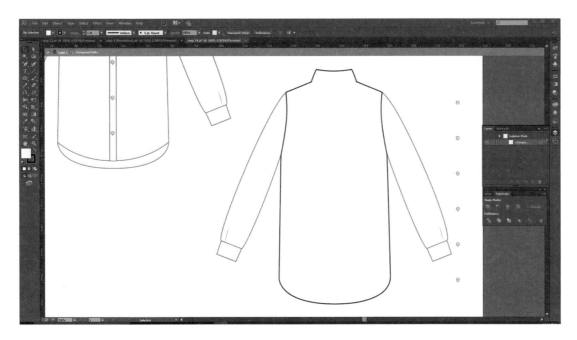

STEP 2

Enter Isolation mode by double clicking and get rid of all elements that you won't need for the back of the shirt—placket, pocket and unnecessary stitching. Leave the buttons on the pasteboard because you will use them later. Leave the hem stitching if you wish, but don't select when uniting. Using the Pathfinder tool, unite all the parts of your shirt: back of the shirt with the bodice, yoke with the bodice, and collar with the bodice. Clean up any stray anchor points that remain, as sometimes a little tidy up is necessary. Send the united shirt bodice to the back, **Arrange > Send to Back**, in order for the hem stitching to appear in front again.

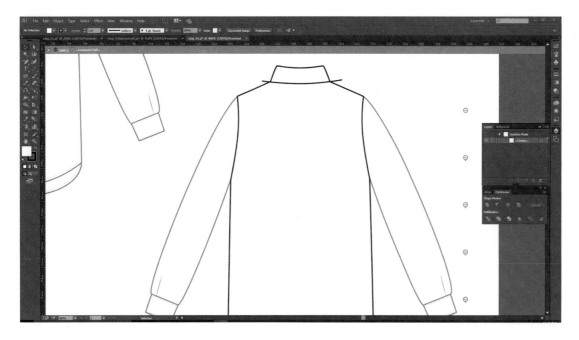

STEP 3

Draw the collar line so it begins and ends
outside the shape. Go to Pathfinder and
select both the line and the shirt bodice
and Divide. Ungroup. Make sure that the
line you draw has no fill or the Divide won't
work. Add the stitching to the back collar.

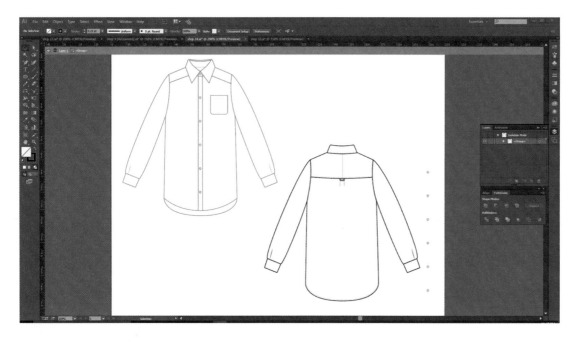

STEP 4

Repeat the process from Step 3 to create
the back yoke. Add the stitching and any
other details.

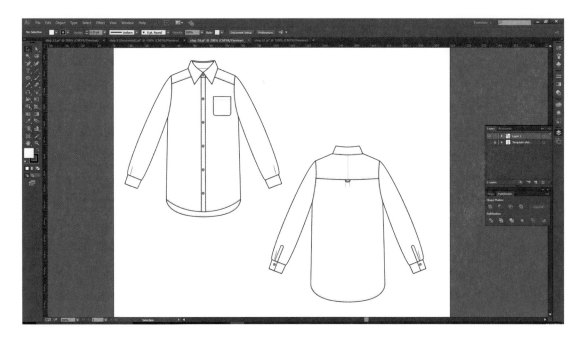

STEP 5

Create the sleeve placket using the Rectangle tool and a combination of Pen tools. Add the stitching. Delete all the buttons that you've saved except one, which you'll need to add to your placket.

Rotate your placket until it fits with your sleeve. When happy, Reflect the placket to the other sleeve.

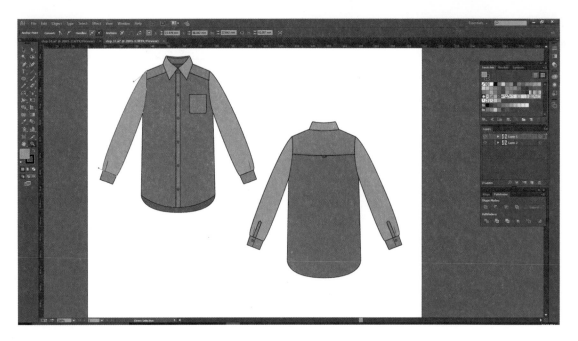

FILL WITH COLOR AND PATTERN

STEP 1

The shirt is now complete. You can fill in
your shirt by Direct Selecting individual
parts that you want to color.

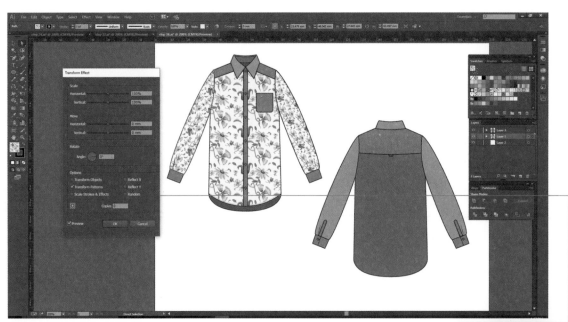

STEP 2

Fill in your shirt with pattern using the
Swatch Library, or create or import your
own patterns. You can also scale, move,
and rotate the patterns. Go to **Effect
> Distort and Transform Effect >
Transform**. The new menu will appear.

Uncheck Transform Objects (make sure
Transform Patterns remains checked) in
the Transform Effect window and check
Preview so that you can see the changes
you're making.

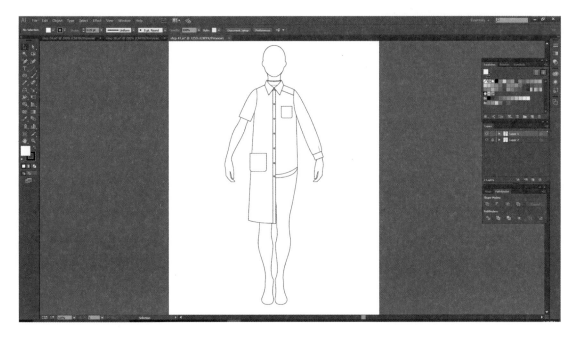

SPEED DESIGNING

STEP 1

You can now use the shirt you've created to speed design, quickly transforming it into a shirt dress. You can work in Isolation mode, adjusting the components you will use and getting rid of any unnecessary parts. Work on half of your garment until you are happy with what you're doing.

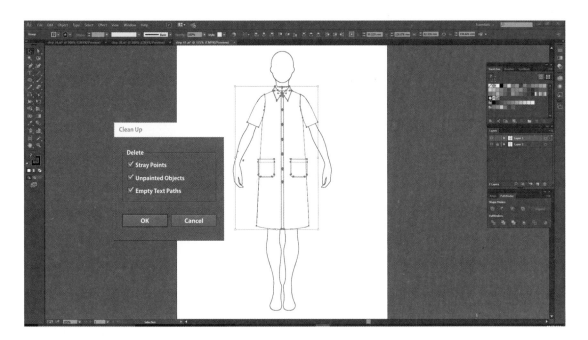

STEP 2

Group all the elements of your shirt dress and Reflect. Add any other details you would like to complete your new garment. Go to **Object > Path > Clean Up** and check OK to delete any stray points that might have been left behind.

Hints and tips

WHAT TO INCLUDE AND WHAT NOT TO INCLUDE

Flats should include only the essential details. If you are drawing from an existing garment, do not draw any wrinkles or flaws in the fabric or construction. Apply a little "cosmetic surgery" and draw only what is necessary. Look at the flats in the second half of this book to gain an idea of what to include and what to leave out. Below are some basic hints and tips addressing mistakes commonly found in technical drawing, using some classic styles as guidelines. Think about the 3D form of the human body and how a garment may need to be cut to fit and be comfortable. An understanding of pattern cutting and garment construction will greatly assist you with this.

Above all, don't imagine or "make up" how details on the garment should look. If you are unsure about how to draw something, it is best to find an existing garment and draw what you see from that, using its details as a guide. Don't draw flaws or mistakes.

Avoid overemphasizing details that might turn the style into something else. Don't be tempted to make your drawing "prettier" with swirly or fancy lines—leave that for your final fashion illustration.

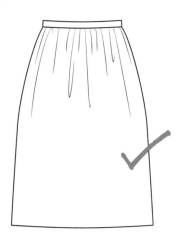

Finally, avoid the urge to get carried away with your own artistic interpretation. Flats are not the place for self-expression. The purpose behind a technical drawing is to convey information as simply, clearly, and accurately as possible. Drawing a skirt as the one above, right, runs the risk of the pattern cutter interpreting this as a wavy hem.

BASIC HINTS AND TIPS FOR DRAWING GARMENTS

If ever you are unsure of how a garment should be drawn, find something similar and check.

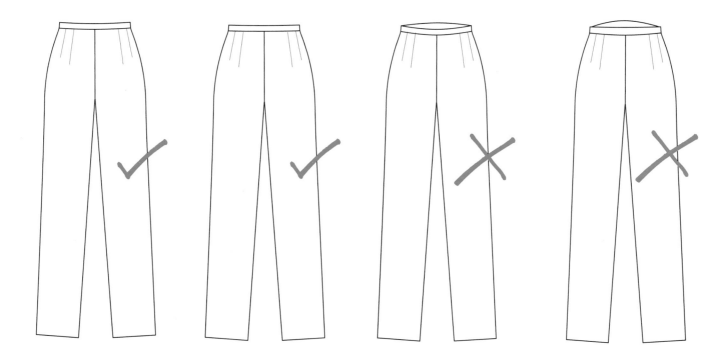

Pants are usually straight at the top. Do not draw overly concave or convex waistbands.

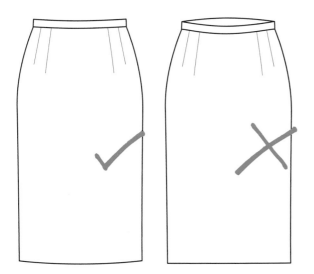

The waistband of a skirt should usually be drawn gently curved.

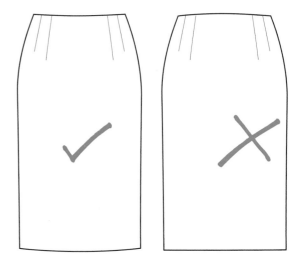

The hem of a skirt should also be drawn gently curved.

A basic back neck will usually be gently curved, to allow for comfort and neck movement. A common mistake is to draw it straight across or concave.

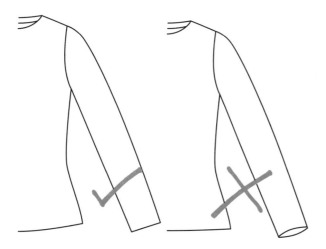 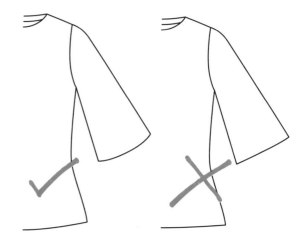

Hems are often drawn curved, but you should only draw a curved hem if that's how you intend it to be. For narrow sleeves (above) and pants (below), the hem should be drawn straight. For wider styles, curve the hem gently.

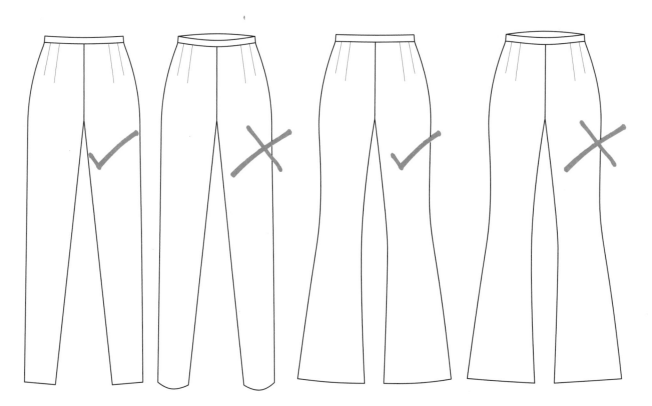

A common mistake is to draw the collar as if it is disconnected from the shoulder seam.

The backs of shirt collars should be gently curved inward: they should never be drawn straight across or exaggeratedly concave or convex.

ALWAYS use one template when working on a body of work, as this will ensure that tops and bottoms remain in proportion to one another. If you reduce or enlarge a drawing at any time, make a note of the percentage, so that everything can be brought back to the same size. Imagine that all your drawings are to fit the same figure, so they should all be in proportion.

DRAWING STYLE/DESIGN DETAILS

The directory in the second half of this book is offered as a guide to interpreting 3D garments, styling details, and hardware in 2D form. There are some conventions for indicating difficult-to-draw or partially hidden details—such as the crotch area on trousers or a concealed zipper—on flats. Those offered in this book are one interpretation, but as long as you follow the basic guidelines for technical drawing, you can develop your own versions.

Though subtly different, these three flats show different but equally correct ways of drawing the front crotch on a pair of pants.

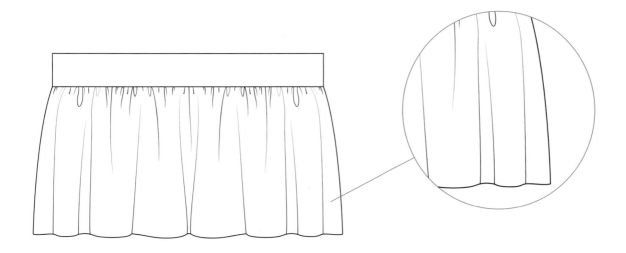

Flare is often difficult to draw—again, to be accurate, use an existing garment and lay it out, focusing on the flared hem, and draw what you see. Give a sense of style movement and drape of the fabric.

There are two ways of drawing gathers. It helps to use a finer line for these delicate details. Depending on the fullness of the gathers, additional lines (above right) may be added.

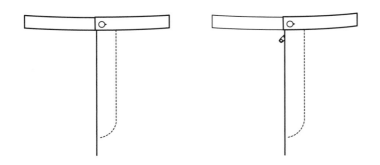

Fly fronts may be drawn with or without the zipper "pull," indicated near left.

Side zippers are usually fairly well concealed, so indicate them with a zipper "pull" and/or a small diagonal stitch. Never draw in the actual teeth of the zipper.

DRAWING INTERNAL, DIFFICULT-TO-SEE, AND HIDDEN DETAILS

Sometimes it is necessary to show the interior of a garment, particularly if the specification includes any detailing on the inside —a colored or fancy lining, or internal stitching, for example.

In these cases you should draw either from the existing garment, or if none exists and you are unsure what to do, find a similar garment, lay it out flat and open the section you wish to see.

An "open" garment would accompany a front view on a spec sheet, a line board, or a design presentation sheet.

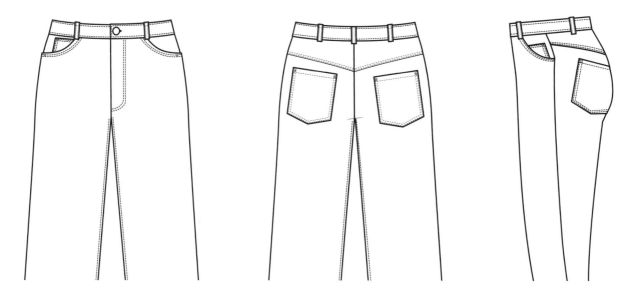

Sometimes detailing travels from front to back over a side seam, or is set in a side seam, so an additional view — such as this side view — may be required.

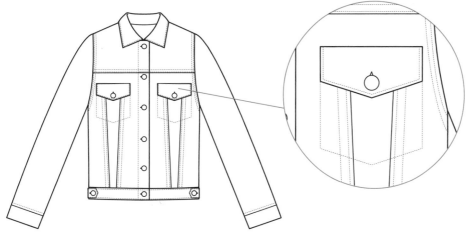

Sometimes tiny details need to be magnified, for example if they are being shown on a spec sheet. Enlarge the required area and show it next to the drawing.

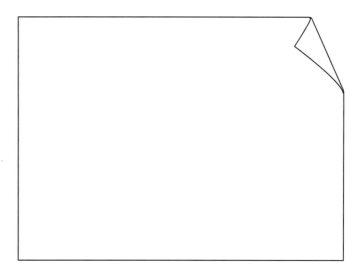

Sometimes you may wish to show a garment unfastened as well as fastened. A sarong, for example, may just be a rectangle of fabric when unfastened and placed flat on the floor, so draw it as such.

Sometimes it is necessary to show the detail on the back of a sleeve. Draw it as if it is folded over. If you are drawing by hand, photocopy your finished drawing, then cut out the drawing carefully. Fold the sleeve section and redraw the placket or detailing, then photocopy the amended drawing and use it like an original.

DRAWING OUTERWEAR

When using the generic template to draw a close-fitting style, you should fit the garment to the outline and shape of the template. Outerwear, however, needs to be drawn slightly larger than the template as, naturally, these garments are worn over other garments.

For ultimate accuracy, if you are working on a coordinated line and need to present all drawings on a line board, you may use the generic template with, for example, a dress, then draw the coat or jacket over this to ensure correct proportions.

DRAWING VERY DETAILED GARMENTS

If you need to draw a very detailed style and are working by hand, first produce the basic garment with all seams. Enlarge the drawing on a photocopier and, using a fine-line pen, add in top stitching and fine detail. Reduce the drawing on a photocopier once it is complete, and the detailing and stitching will be intricate and accurately represented. You may also want to show enlarged images of particularly detailed or elaborate sections for clarity.

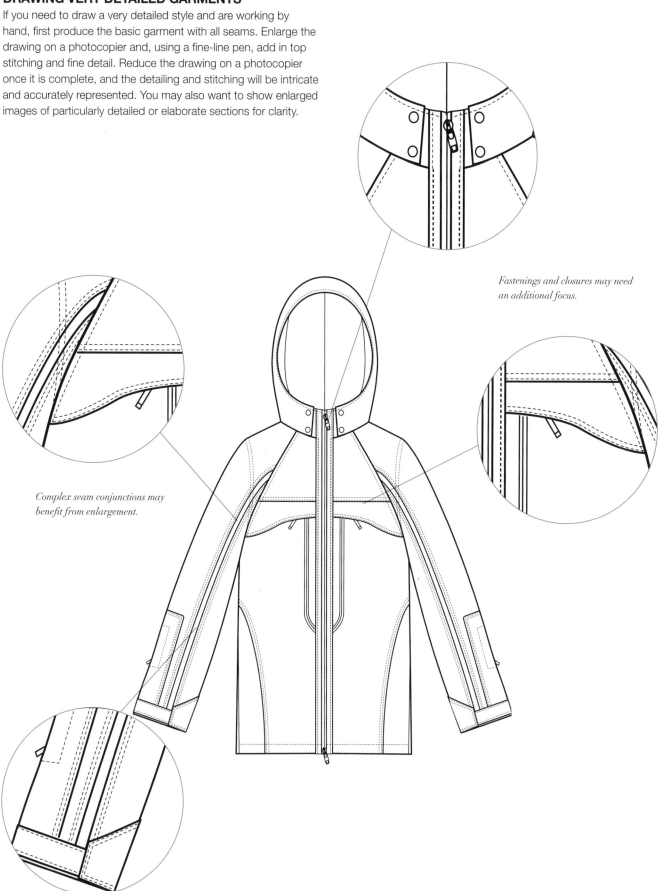

Fastenings and closures may need an additional focus.

Complex seam conjunctions may benefit from enlargement.

PATTERN

When applying print or pattern to a style, pay attention to where the seams and gathers are, as these will cause a break in the pattern. Do not simply lay a pattern flat over a garment, as it would not look this way in real life. You also need to consider the scale of your print pattern to ensure an accurate representation.

TEXTURE

Unless the texture of a fabric is very different (fake fur, for example), the technical drawing will generally be unaffected. Texture will occasionally vary the line of a flat, as seen in the example below: the style is shown as though it were made in a simple cotton (left), and then in a short-pile fake-fur fabric (right).

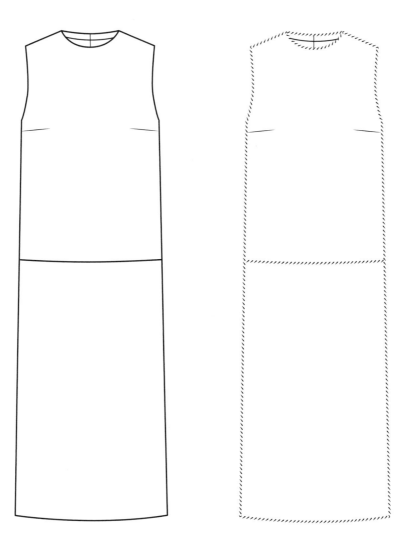

Different drawing styles

It is inevitable that your flats will be in your own specific style. As long as the drawings are clear, detailed, and in proportion, it is acceptable that they retain your own personal signature.

Shown here are a number of interpretations by different hands of the same single-breasted jacket. Note the differences as well as the similarities. We all see things differently; however, the key to creating successful flats is an understanding of proportion, styling, and garment construction.

Design details

To produce a flat, a knowledge of basic styling information may be used as a guide. The outlines on the following pages are a reminder of terminology and the standard elements for a skirt, pants, shirt, and jacket. The diagrams on pages 72–75 show how to interpret different sleeve, dress, skirt, pants, and coat lengths on the generic template.

BASIC SKIRT

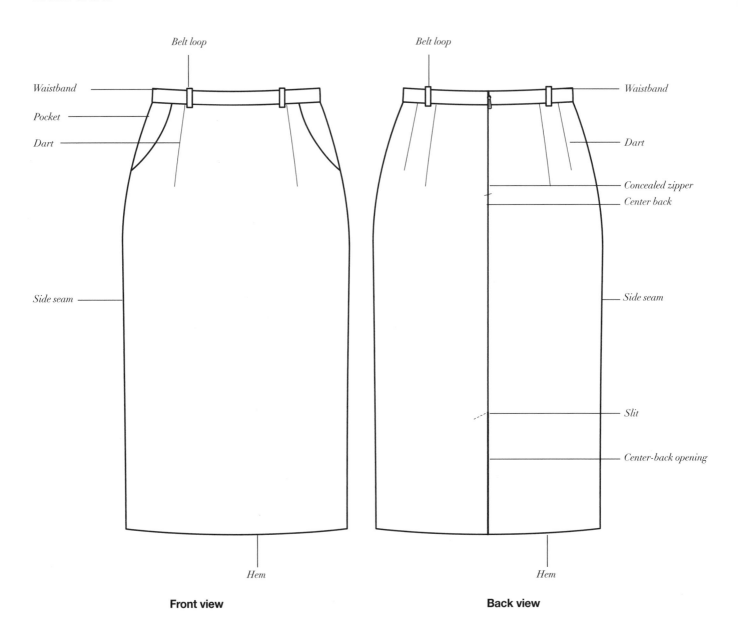

Front view

Back view

BASIC PANTS

Fly front showing internal detail

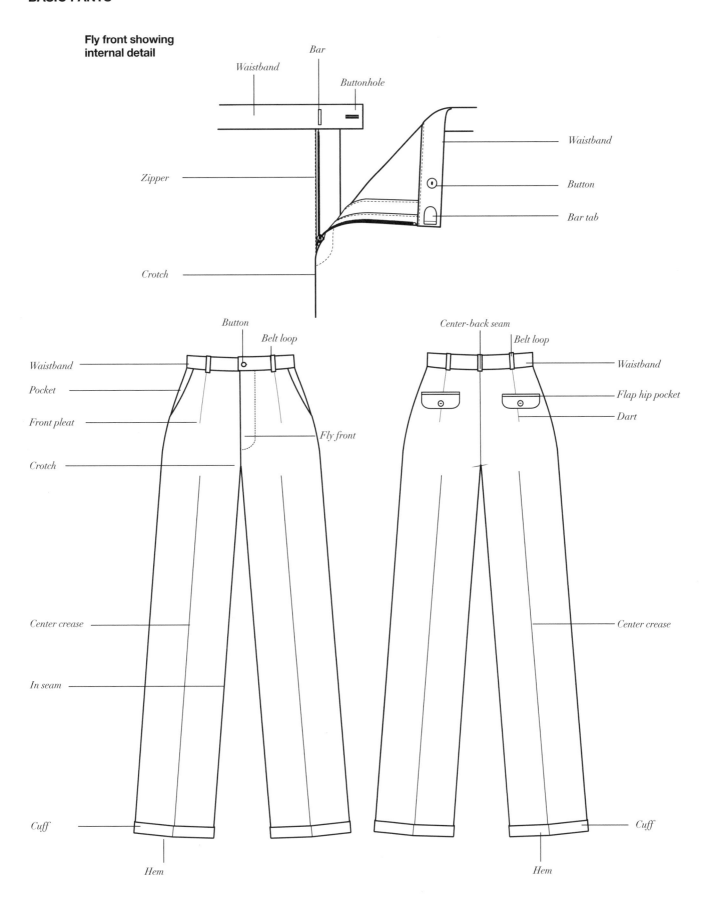

Bar

Waistband

Buttonhole

Waistband

Zipper

Button

Bar tab

Crotch

Button

Center-back seam

Belt loop

Belt loop

Waistband

Waistband

Flap hip pocket

Pocket

Front pleat

Dart

Fly front

Crotch

Center crease

Center crease

In seam

Cuff

Cuff

Hem

Hem

Front view

Back view

BASIC SHIRT

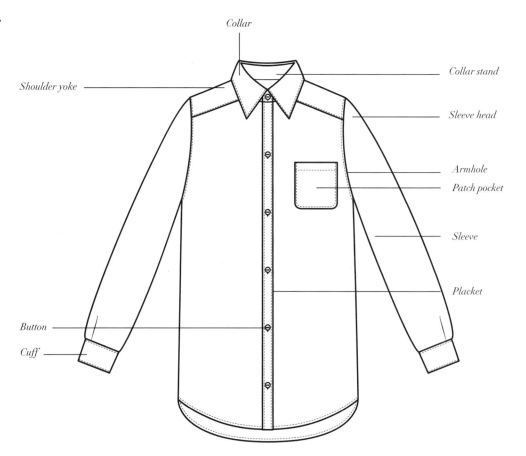

Collar

Shoulder yoke

Collar stand

Sleeve head

Armhole

Patch pocket

Sleeve

Placket

Button

Cuff

Front view

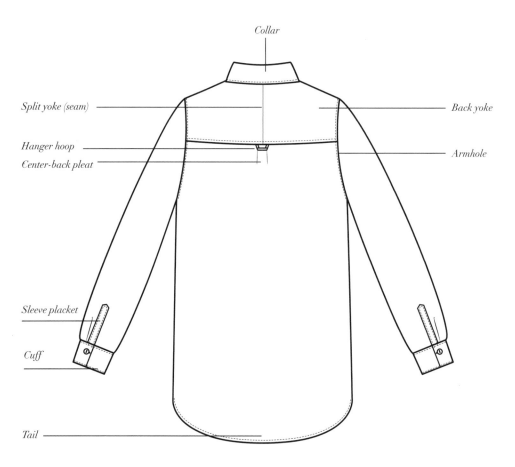

Collar

Split yoke (seam)

Back yoke

Hanger hoop

Armhole

Center-back pleat

Sleeve placket

Cuff

Tail

Back view

BASIC JACKET

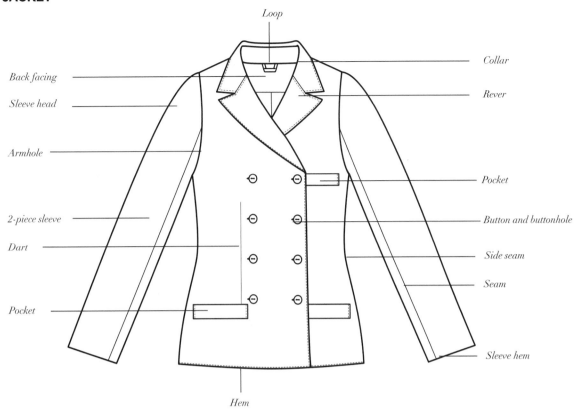

Loop

Collar

Back facing

Rever

Sleeve head

Armhole

Pocket

2-piece sleeve

Button and buttonhole

Dart

Side seam

Seam

Pocket

Sleeve hem

Hem

Front view

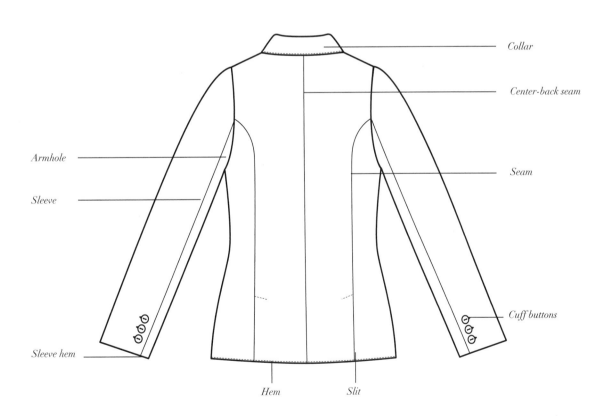

Collar

Center-back seam

Armhole

Seam

Sleeve

Cuff buttons

Sleeve hem

Hem   Slit

Back view

SLEEVE LENGTHS

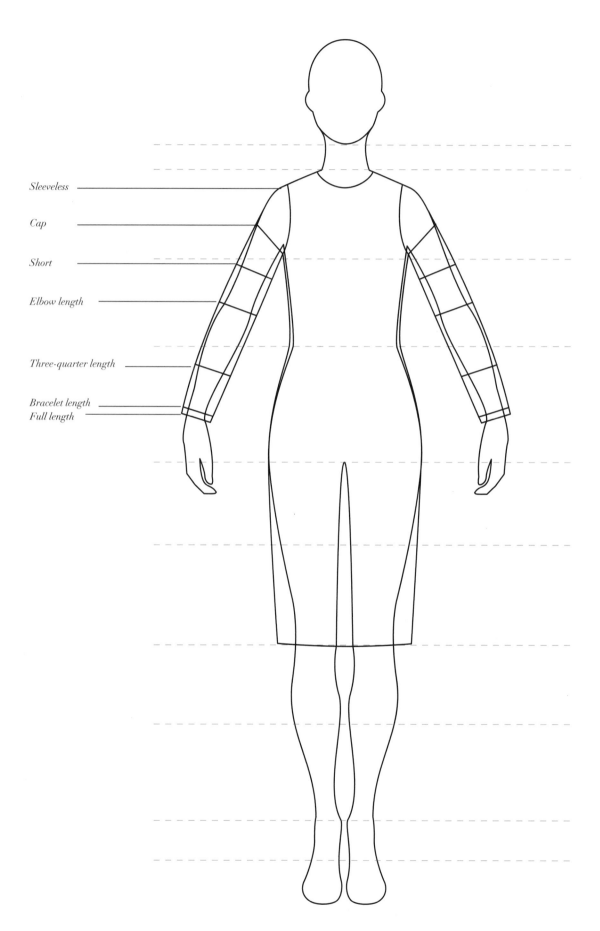

Sleeveless

Cap

Short

Elbow length

Three-quarter length

Bracelet length
Full length

DRESS AND SKIRT LENGTHS

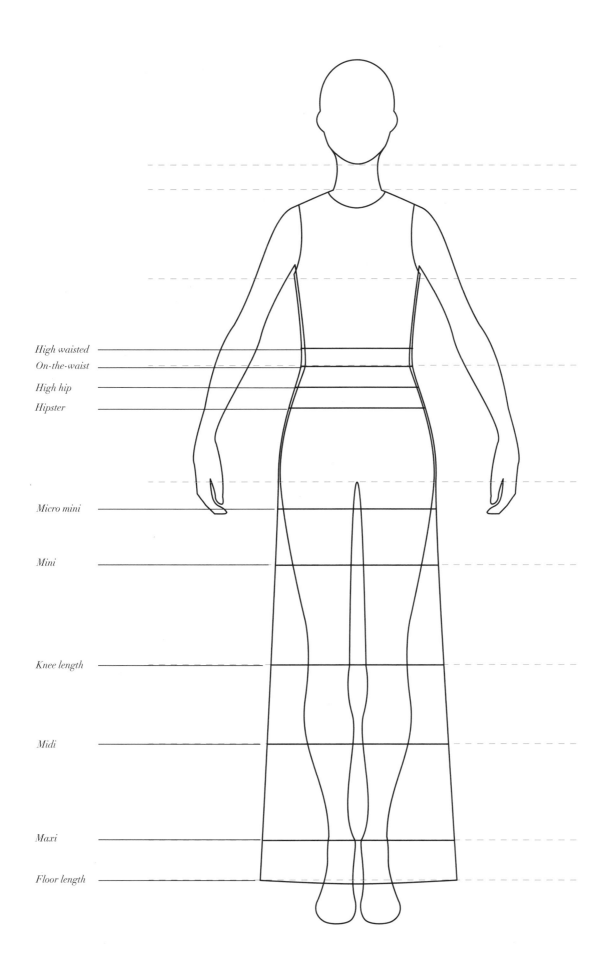

High waisted

On-the-waist

High hip

Hipster

Micro mini

Mini

Knee length

Midi

Maxi

Floor length

PANTS LENGTHS

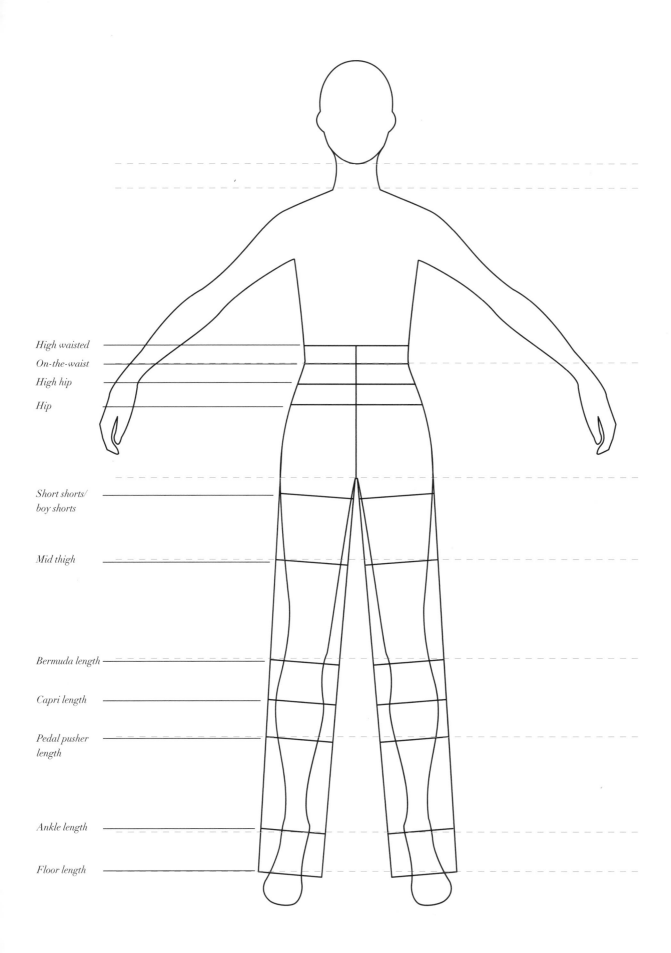

High waisted

On-the-waist

High hip

Hip

Short shorts/
boy shorts

Mid thigh

Bermuda length

Capri length

Pedal pusher
length

Ankle length

Floor length

COAT LENGTHS

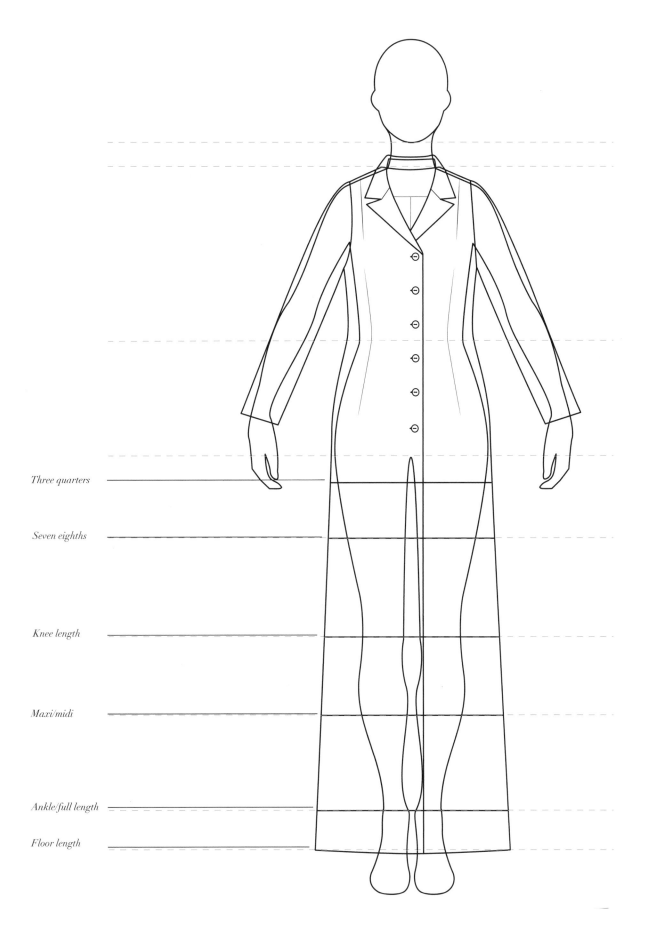

Three quarters

Seven eighths

Knee length

Maxi/midi

Ankle/full length

Floor length

VISUAL DIRECTORY
OF STYLES
AND DETAILS

Using the Directory

This section of the book provides a selection of key womenswear shapes and garments. The main garment groups have been researched and analyzed to create a core collection of generic known styles. "Fashion" elements have been erased, where possible, to create generic styles with the minimum of distracting details.

This directory is intended as a guide to the most basic, classic styles and details that can be adapted and developed into your own design ideas. There are myriad other dress, jacket, collar, skirt, and pants styles to choose from, but those featured here are the most well known.

Each garment group begins with a selection of key basic shapes, which are each shown as a simple muslin and as a flat to demonstrate how a three-dimensional garment can translate into a two-dimensional drawing. You will learn how to visualize a garment in two dimensions, and see what needs to be left in and what should be taken out. Developing a good eye is key to producing a successful flat that truly replicates a desired garment design and provides essential information for anyone that looks at it.

Each style has been given the most commonly used name in industry, and you will see that sometimes there are a number of names or definitions for the same style. Understanding and becoming familiar with terminology will help you to "speak fashion" and provide you with additional knowledge.

It is essential to become familiar with generic garments and their key components in order to develop your own styles. Try producing 100 versions of a single-breasted jacket or a double-breasted coat using your knowledge of silhouettes that are functional. Consider sleeve types, collar options, and style lines. The possibilities are endless. By starting with understood basics, you will easily and fluidly progress to creating new, undefined styles.

Go to the womenswear department of any department store, where you can make notes with ease, and see how many "classic" collars, sleeves, cuffs, skirts, and dress silhouettes you can find and look at the multitude of variations. You will see that most garments fall into the categories listed in this section of the book. Almost everything you will see is a variation on a generic style.

Try an experiment: using the generic template, consider how you would create a "new" style. What will the overall silhouette be? What kind of a sleeve will it have? What about a cuff? Consider a collar. How long will it be? Combine the different elements, using the basic styles as a foundation on which to build. Design is all about variation—you will find the art of design development, as well as drawing, easier to get to grips with if you possess the building blocks.

This section provides all the information you need to get started.

FITTED/SHEATH
Front view

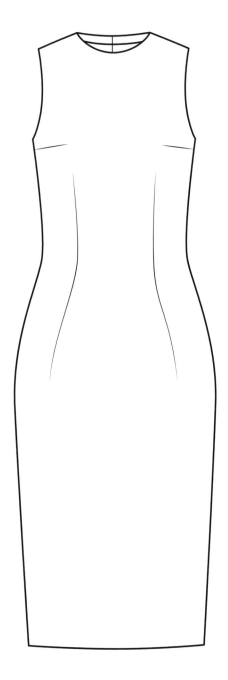

Dresses

FITTED/SHEATH
Back view

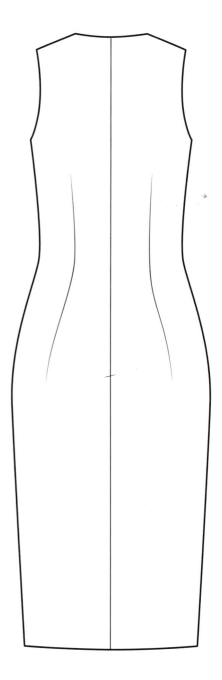

SHIFT/TANK/CHEMISE
Front view

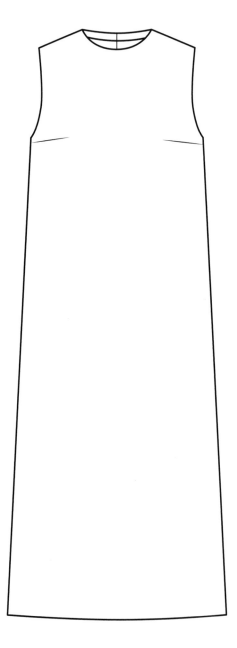

SHIFT/TANK/CHEMISE
Back view

A-LINE
Front view

Dresses

A-LINE
Back view

EMPIRE LINE
Front views

PRINCESS/PRINCESS LINE

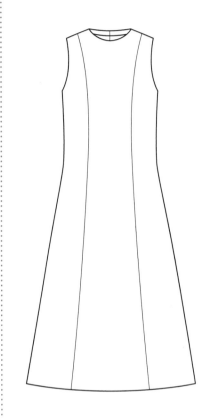

TRAPEZE

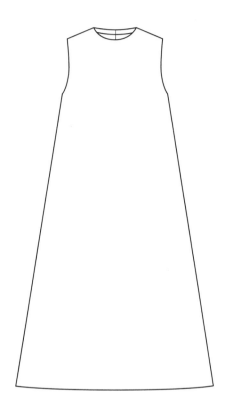

Back views

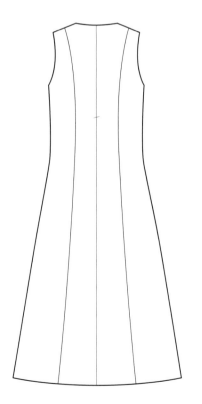

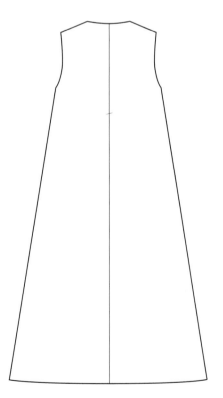

Dresses

ASYMMETRIC
Front views

DROPPED WAIST/DROP WAIST

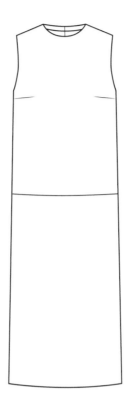

BLOUSON

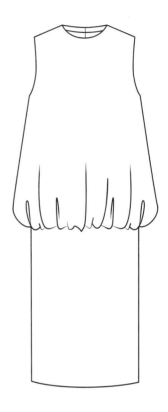

Back views

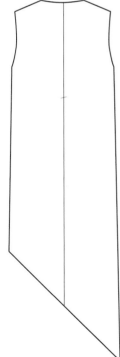

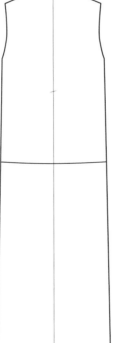

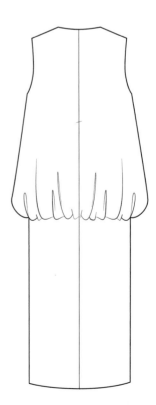

SMOCK
Front views

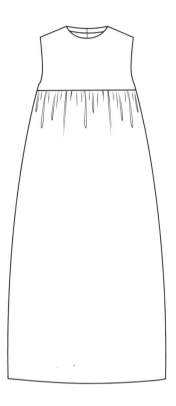

WRAPOVER/WRAP DRESS

Back views

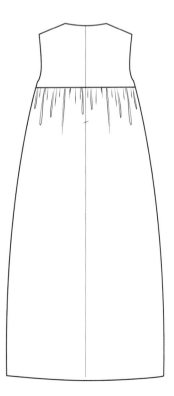

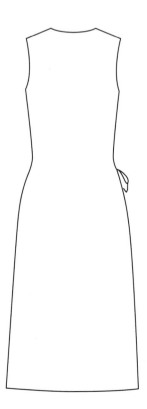

Dresses

SHIRT DRESS/SHIRT WAIST

Front views

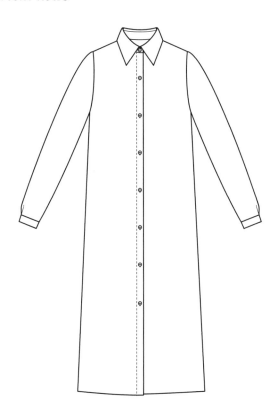

CHEONGSAM/CHINESE DRESS

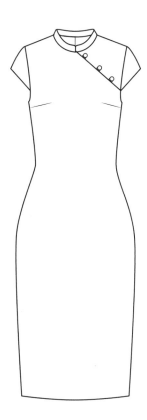

Back views

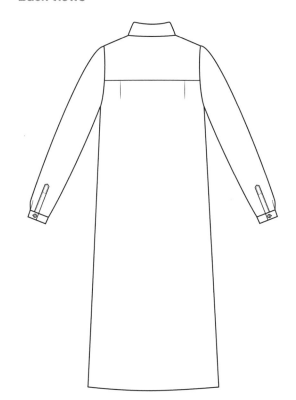

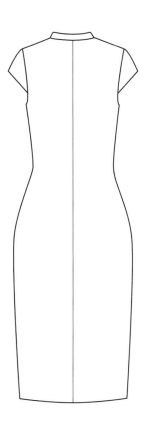

APRON/PINAFORE

Front views

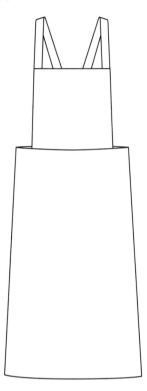

KIMONO

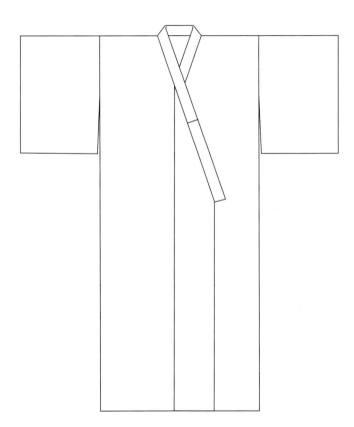

Back views

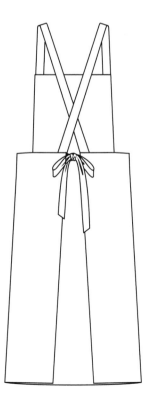

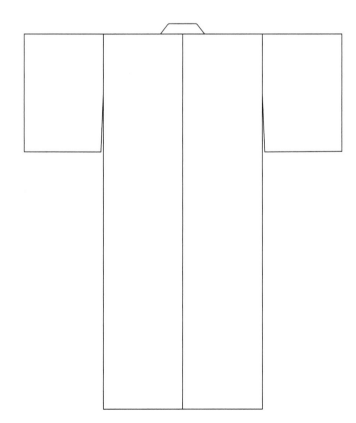

Dresses

KAFTAN
Front views

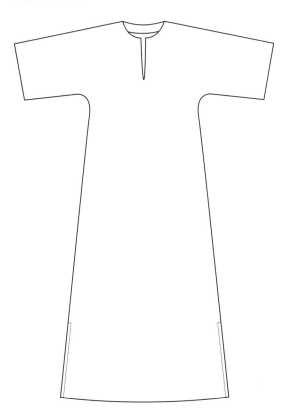

Back views

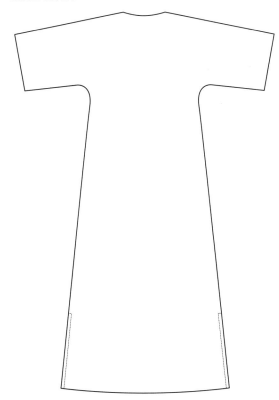

BALL GOWN/GOWN/PROM DRESS

PENCIL SKIRT/FITTED SKIRT/SHEATH

Front view

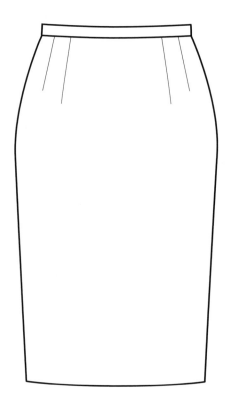

Skirts

PENCIL SKIRT/FITTED SKIRT/SHEATH
Back view

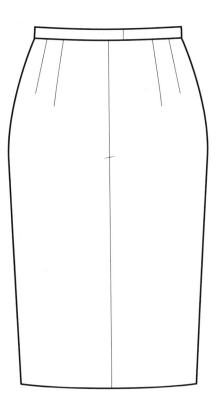

STRAIGHT SKIRT
Front view

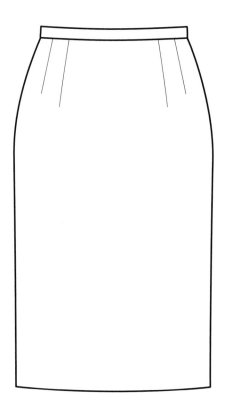

Skirts

STRAIGHT SKIRT
Back view

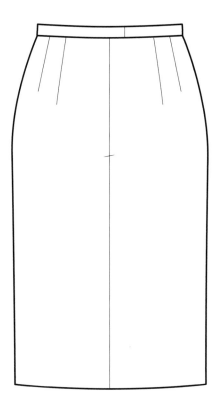

A-LINE SKIRT
Front view

Skirts

A-LINE SKIRT
Back view

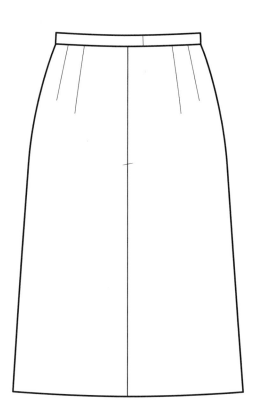

CIRCULAR/FULL CIRCLE SKIRT
Front view

Skirts

CIRCULAR/FULL CIRCLE SKIRT
Back view

GATHERED SKIRT
Front view

Skirts

GATHERED SKIRT
Back view

 **Skirts**

PLEATED SKIRT
Front view

PLEATED SKIRT
Back view

DIRNDL SKIRT
Front views

GORED/GODET SKIRT

WRAP/WRAPOVER SKIRT

 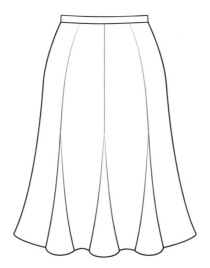 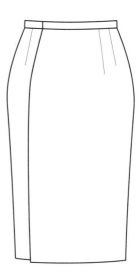

Back views

 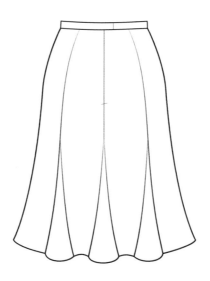 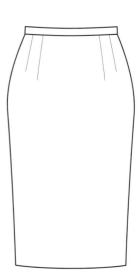

Skirts

SARONG/PAREO
Front views

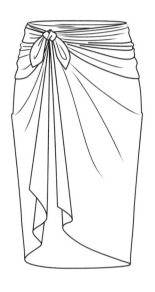

TIERED/GYPSY SKIRT

HANDKERCHIEF HEM/
IRREGULAR HEM SKIRT

Back views

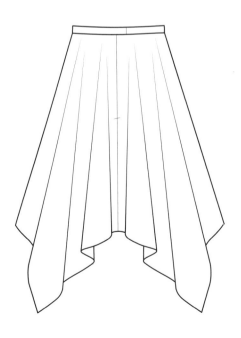

ASYMMETRIC SKIRT
Front views

PUFFBALL/BUBBLE/BALLOON SKIRT

SKATING SKIRT

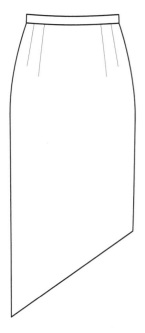

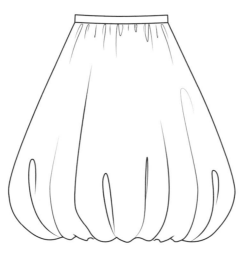

Back views

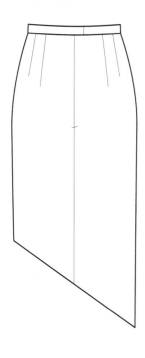

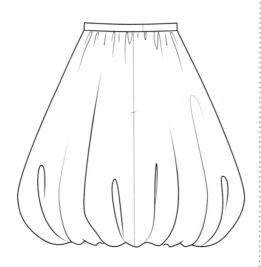

Skirts

KILT
Front views

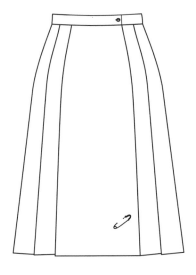

SKORT

PEG/PEGGED/HOBBLE SKIRT

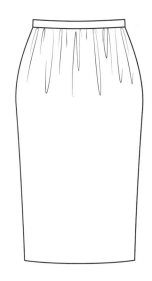

Back views

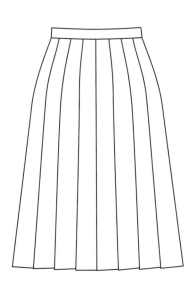

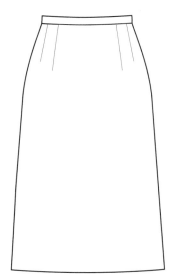

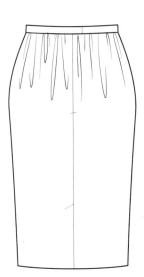

 **Pants**

LEGGING
Front view

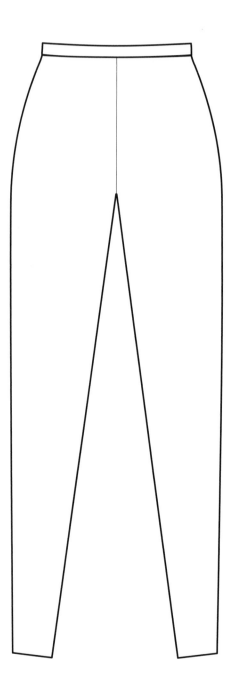

Pants

LEGGING
Back view

 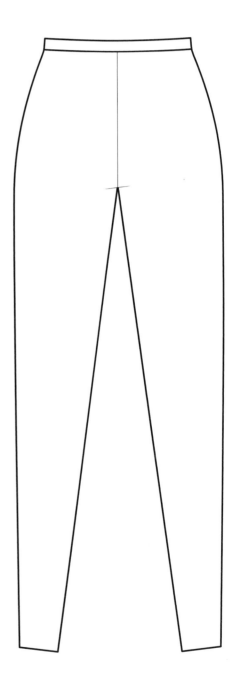

DRAINPIPE/SKINNY/CIGARETTE PANT/STOVEPIPE
Front view

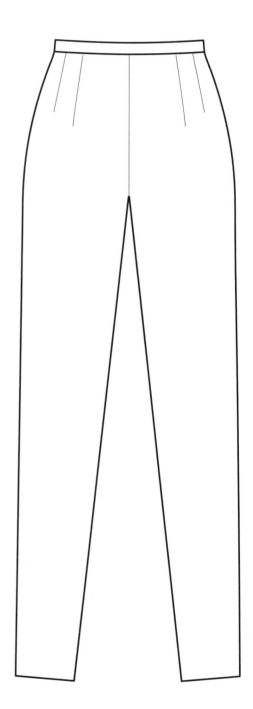

Pants

DRAINPIPE/SKINNY/CIGARETTE PANT/STOVEPIPE
Back view

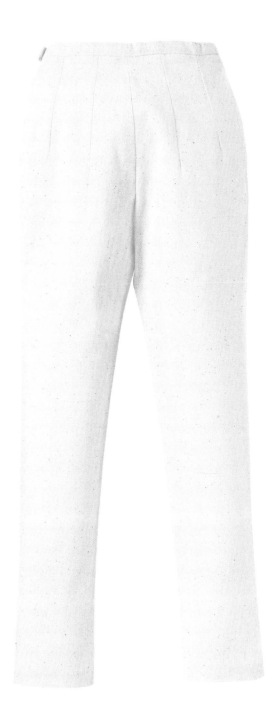

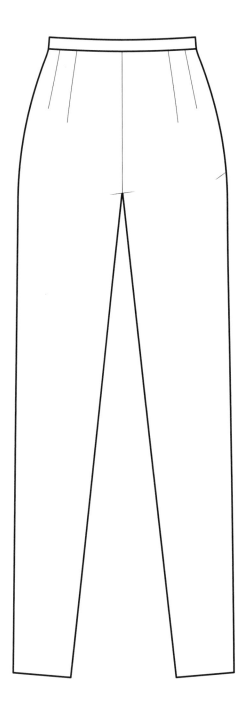

STRAIGHT
Front view

Pants

STRAIGHT
Back view

 **Pants**

TAPERED
Front view

Pants

TAPERED
Back view

BELLBOTTOM/FLARED
Front view

Pants

BELLBOTTOM/FLARED
Back view

Pants

BOOTLEG/BOOTCUT
Front views

JEAN/JEANS

**CARGO PANT/
COMBAT PANT**

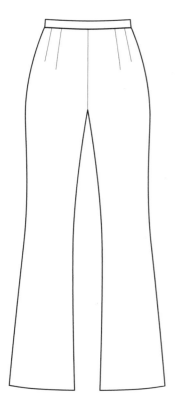

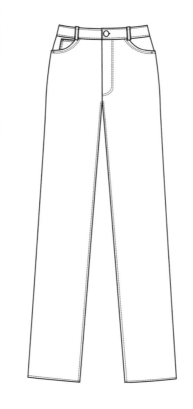

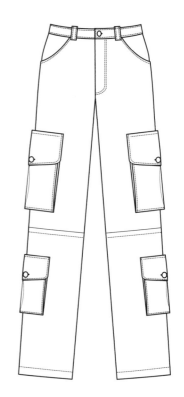

Back views

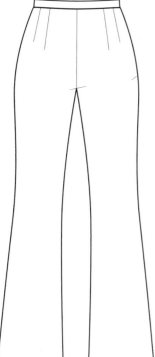

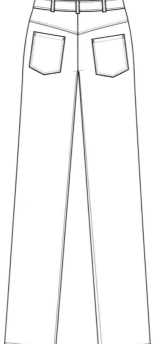

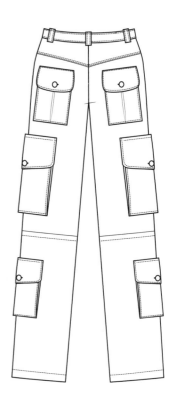

Pants

OXFORD BAG
Front views

**JODHPUR/
RIDING PANT**

PALAZZO PANT

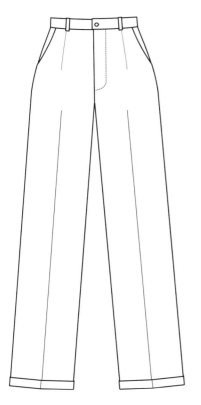

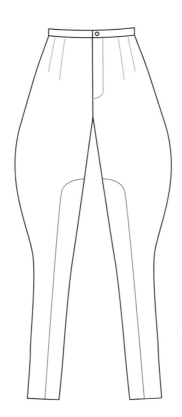

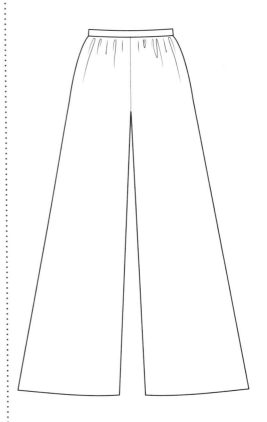

Back views

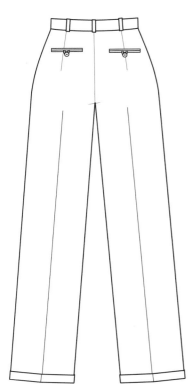

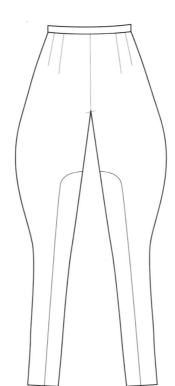

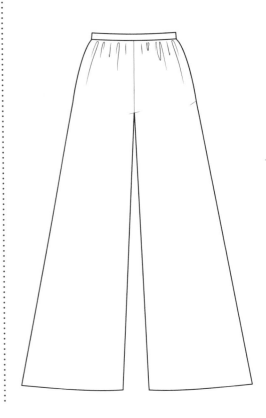

 **Pants**

SAILOR
Front views

HAREM PANT

DHOTI

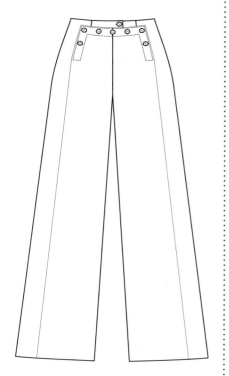

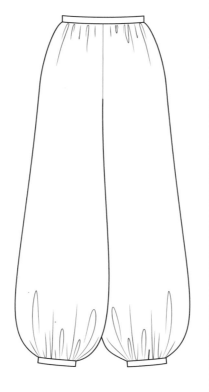

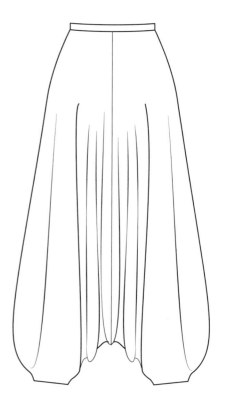

Back views

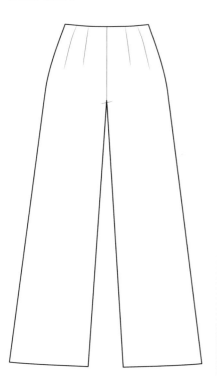

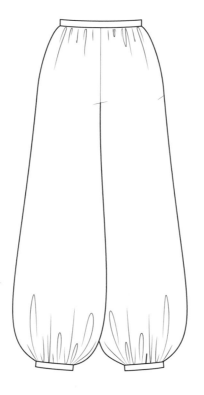

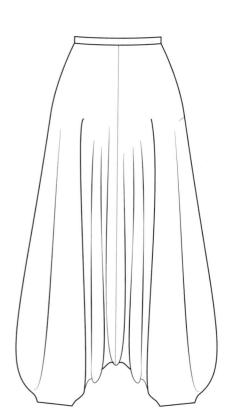

Pants

ZOUAVE

Front views

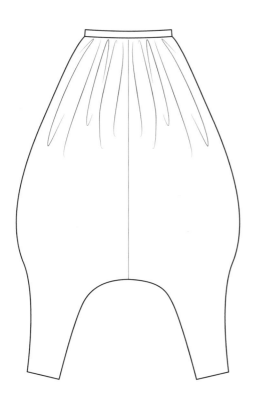

CULOTTE/PANT SKIRT

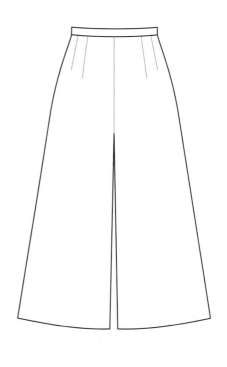

Back views

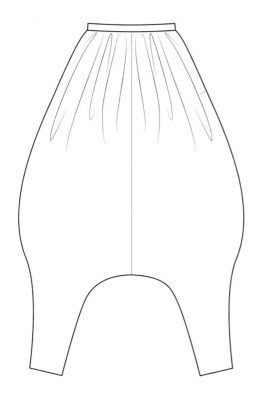

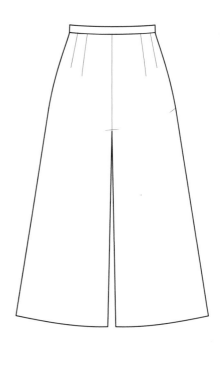

**HOTPANT/MICRO SHORT/
SHORT SHORTS**

BOXER SHORT

BLOOMER

Front views

Back views

Pants

BERMUDA SHORT
Front views

KNICKERBOCKER/KNICKERS

GOUCHO PANT

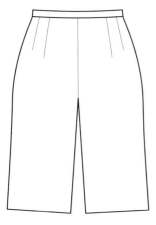

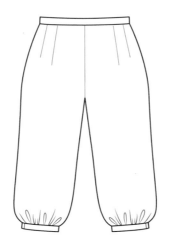

Back views

CAPRI/SABRINA PANT
Front views

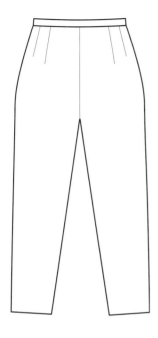

PEDAL PUSHER/CLAM DIGGER

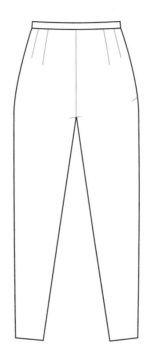

PEG TROUSER

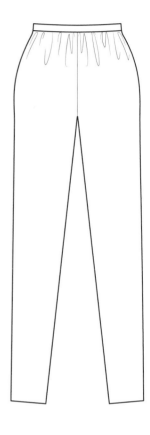

Back views

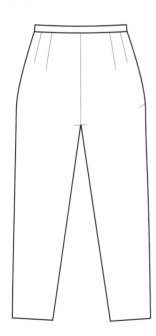

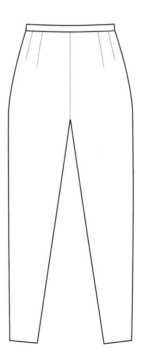

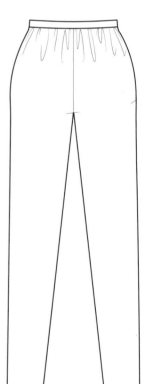

Pants

JOGGER/SWEAT PANT/TRACK PANT

Front views

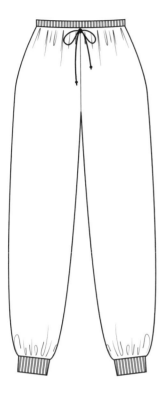

STIRRUP PANT

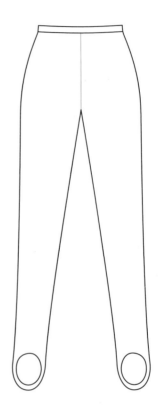

Back views

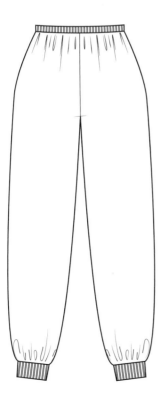

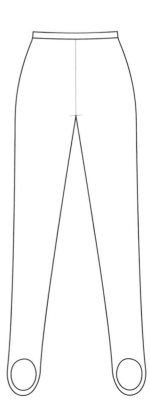

DUNGAREE/BIB OVERALL
Front views

JUMPSUIT/BOILER SUIT/COVERALL

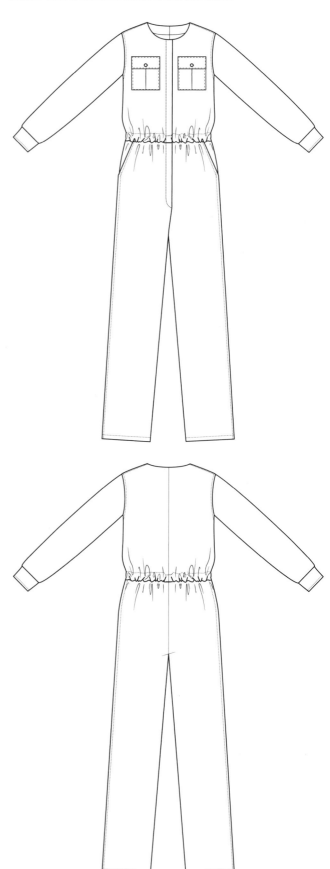

Back views

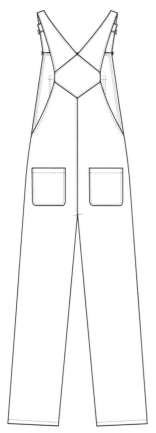

Pants

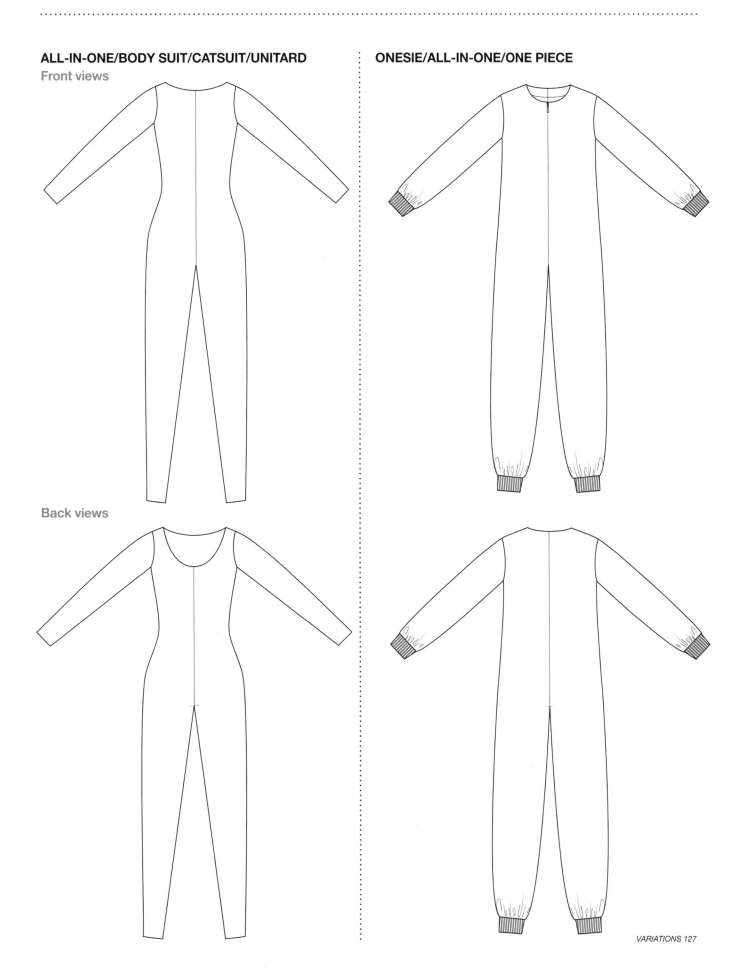

ALL-IN-ONE/BODY SUIT/CATSUIT/UNITARD
Front views

ONESIE/ALL-IN-ONE/ONE PIECE

Back views

CAMISOLE/STRAPPY VEST
Front view

Tops

CAMISOLE/STRAPPY VEST
Back view

 **Tops**

VEST/TANK
Front view

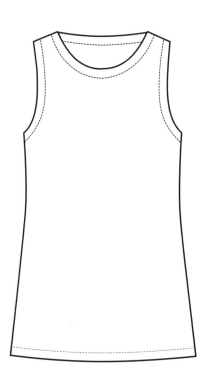

Tops

VEST/TANK
Back view

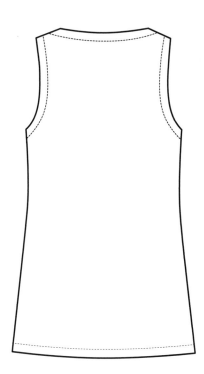

 **Tops**

TUNIC
Front view

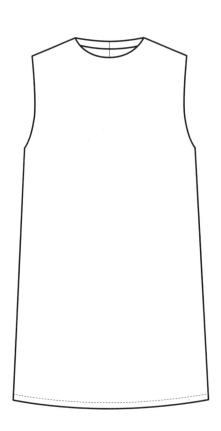

TUNIC
Back view

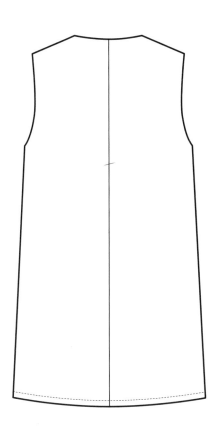

T-SHIRT/TEE
Front view

Tops

T-SHIRT/TEE
Back view

SHIRT
Front view

SHIRT
Back view

 **Tops**

CROP/MIDRIFF TOP
Front views

SLEEVELESS T-SHIRT

WAISTCOAT/VEST

STRAPLESS TOP/ TUBE TOP

Back views

Tops

CARDIGAN/FULLY-FASHIONED KNIT
Front views

BLOUSE

Back views

BUSTIER
Front views

CORSET

HALTER/HALTER NECK

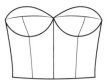

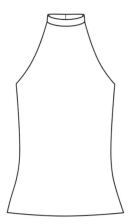

Back views

Tops

COSSACK
Front views

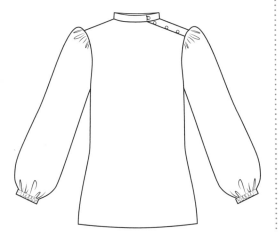

GYPSY/PEASANT BLOUSE

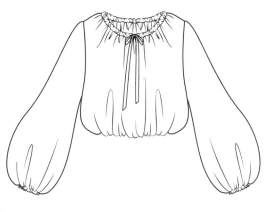

BLOUSON

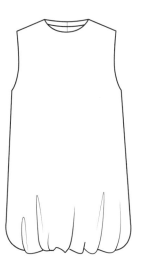

Back views

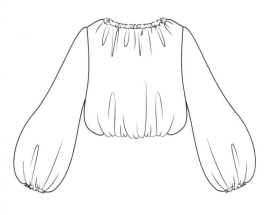

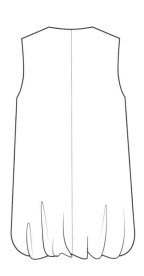

WRAP TOP/BALLET TOP
Front views

KURTA/KURTI

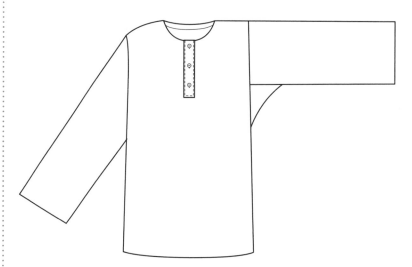

Back views

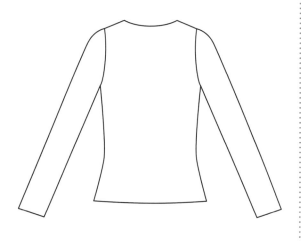

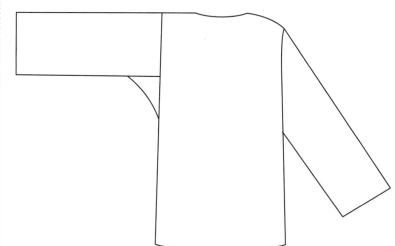

Tops

POLO SHIRT
Front views

**SWEATSHIRT/JOGGING TOP/
SWEAT TOP**

**BODYSUIT/BODY/
LEOTARD**

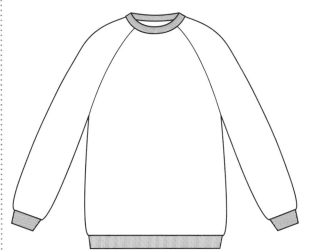

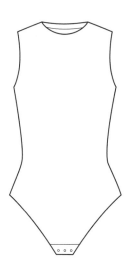

Back views

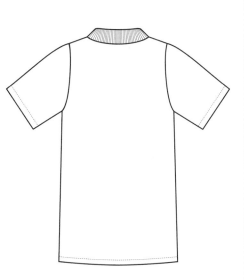

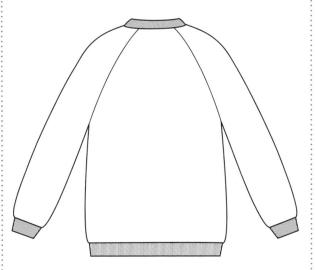

Jackets

CLASSIC SINGLE-BREASTED
Front view

Jackets

CLASSIC SINGLE-BREASTED
Back view

Jackets

CLASSIC DOUBLE-BREASTED
Front view

Jackets

CLASSIC DOUBLE-BREASTED
Back view

Jackets

CASUAL/UNSTRUCTURED/BOXY
Front view

Jackets

CASUAL/UNSTRUCTURED/BOXY
Back view

SHRUG
Front views

BOLERO/MATADOR

SPENCER JACKET

Back views

Jackets

BLAZER/BOX JACKET
Front views

TUXEDO/DINNER JACKET

CHINESE/MANDARIN JACKET

Back views

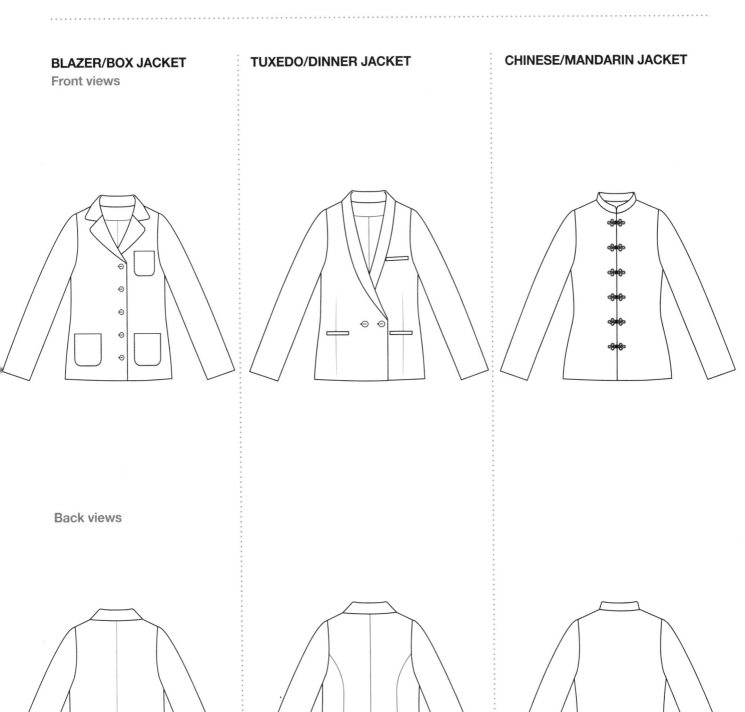

NEHRU JACKET
Front views

SAFARI JACKET

NORFOLK JACKET

Back views

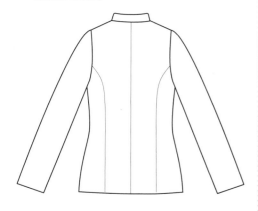

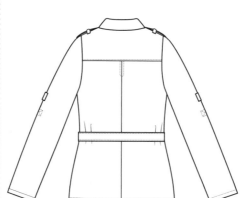

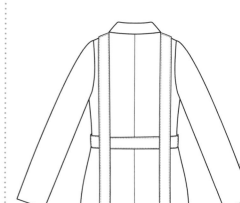

Jackets

BOMBER/BLOUSON/FLIGHT JACKET
Front views

WESTERN/JEAN JACKET

Back views

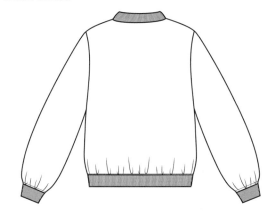

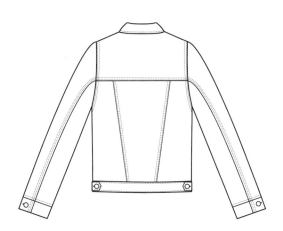

BIKER/MOTORCYCLE JACKET
Front views

WINDCHEATER/CAGOULE

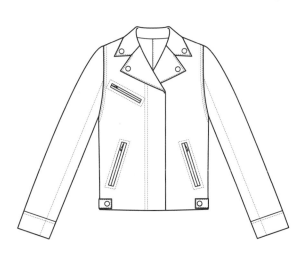

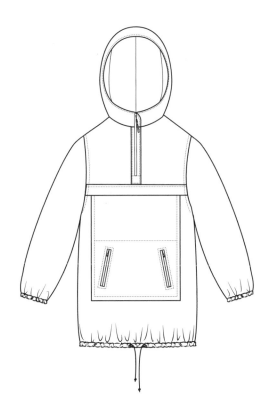

Back views

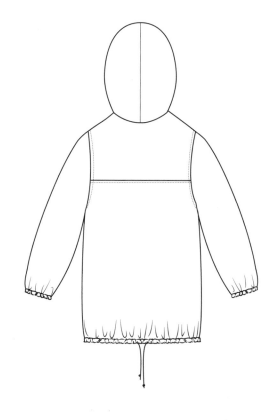

Jackets

**BODY WARMER/PADDED VEST/
QUILTED VEST/PADDED GILET**

Front views

PARKA

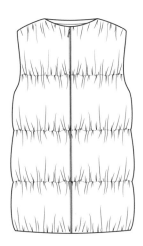

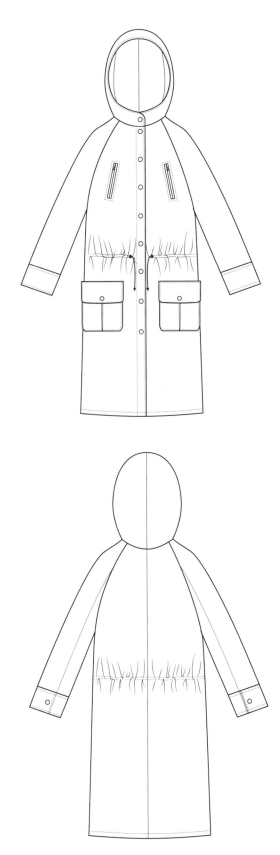

Back views

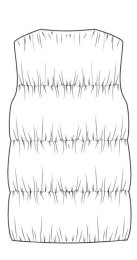

CLASSIC SINGLE-BREASTED
Front view

Coats

CLASSIC SINGLE-BREASTED
Back view

CLASSIC DOUBLE-BREASTED
Front view

CLASSIC DOUBLE-BREASTED
Back view

CASUAL/UNSTRUCTURED
Front view

Coats

CASUAL/UNSTRUCTURED
Back view

PRINCESS/PRINCESS-LINE COAT
Front views

MACKINTOSH/MAC

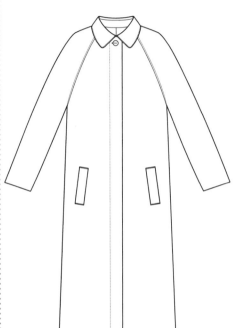

TRENCH COAT

Back views

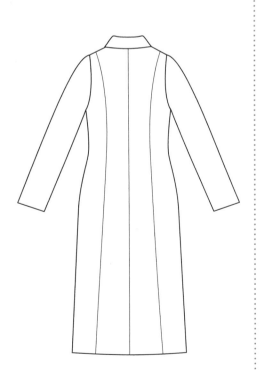

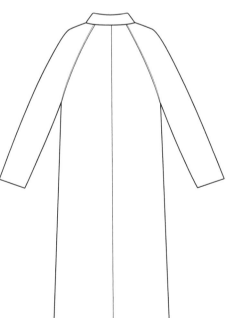

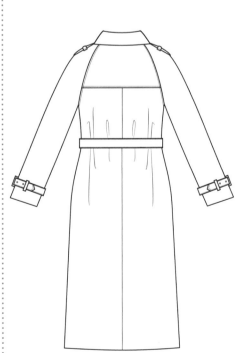

COCOON COAT
Front views

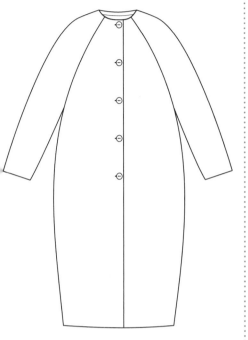

PEA COAT

SWAGGER/TENT/SWING COAT

Back views

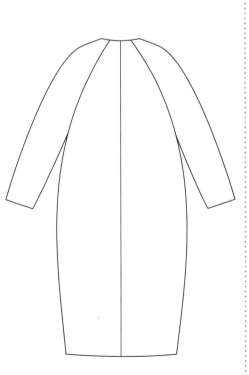

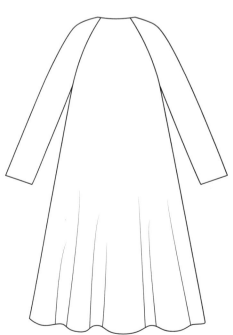

Front views

DUFFLE/TOGGLE COAT

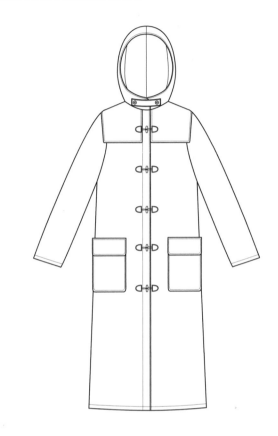

Back views

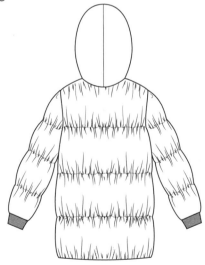

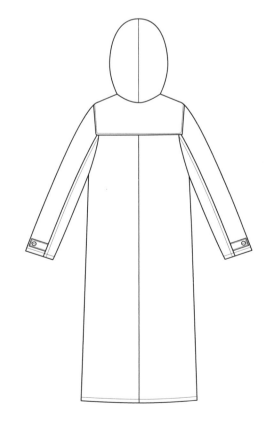

Coats

DUSTER COAT
Front views

CAPE

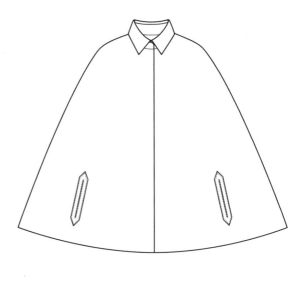

Back views

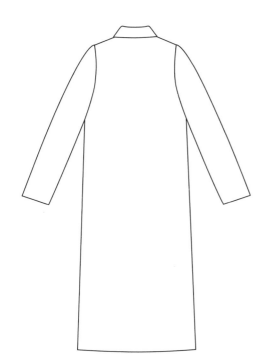

ROUND/JEWEL NECK
Front view

Back view

Necklines

V-NECK

Front view

Back view

U/PLUNGE NECK
Front view

 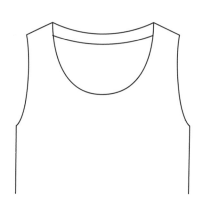

Back view

 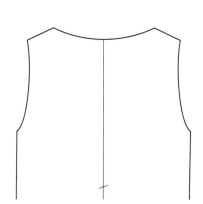

Necklines

SCOOP/SCOOPED NECK
Front view

Back view

BOAT/BATEAU NECK
Front view

Back view

Necklines

SQUARE NECK
Front view

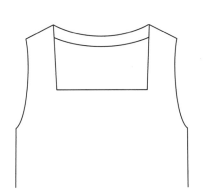

Back view

KEY BASIC SHAPES 171

Necklines

SLIT NECK
Front views   Back views

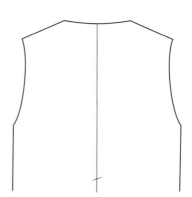

KEYHOLE NECK

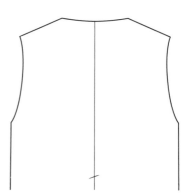

SWEETHEART NECKLINE

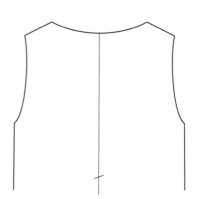

Necklines

ASYMMETRIC NECKLINE

Front views

Back views

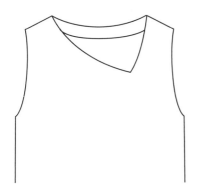 

OFF-THE-SHOULDER

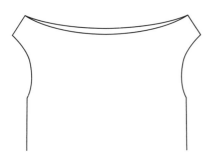 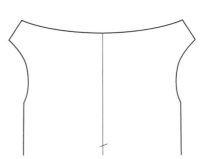

GATHERED NECKLINE

DRAWSTRING NECK

Front views

Back views

CREW NECK

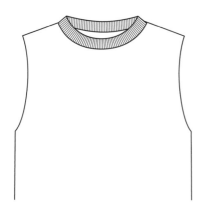
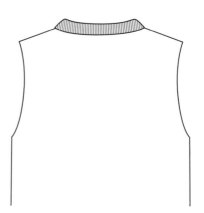

TURTLE/POLO NECK

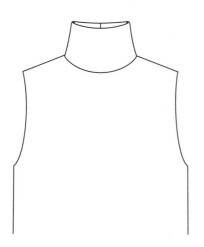

Necklines

FUNNEL NECK/RAISED NECKLINE

Front views   Back views

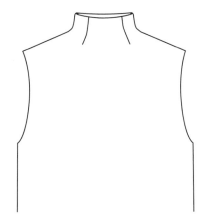
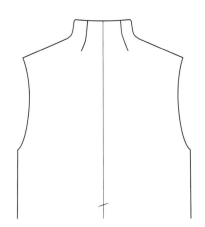

COWL NECK

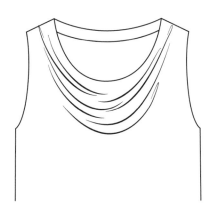
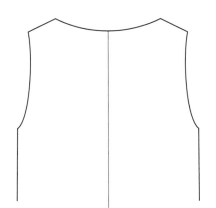

ROLL NECK

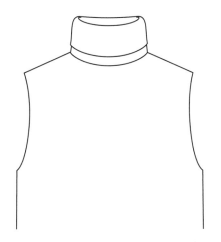

TWO-PIECE SHIRT COLLAR/COLLAR AND BAND/TRADITIONAL/OPEN CONVERTIBLE
Front view

Back view

 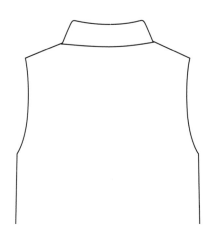

Collars

ONE-PIECE SHIRT COLLAR/CONVERTIBLE COLLAR

Front view

Back view

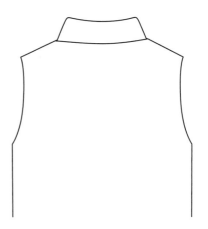

COLLAR AND REVER/NOTCHED COLLAR/TWO-PIECE COLLAR

Front view

Back view

Collars

SHAWL COLLAR

Front view

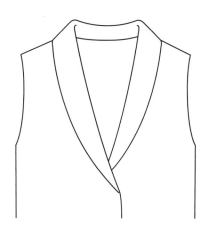

Back view

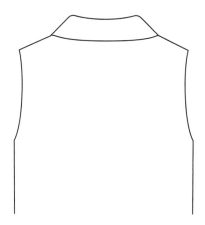

BAND/GRANDAD COLLAR

Front views   Back views

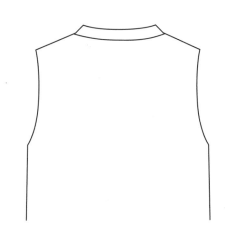

MANDARIN/CHINESE/NEHRU COLLAR

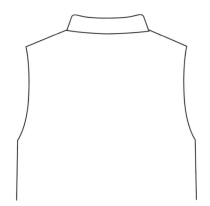

WING COLLAR

Collars

PETER PAN COLLAR

Front views   Back views

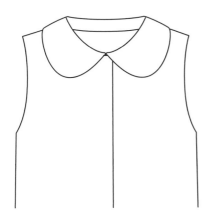 

ETON COLLAR

SAILOR COLLAR

 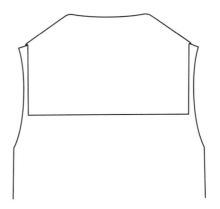

BERTHA COLLAR
Front views

Back views

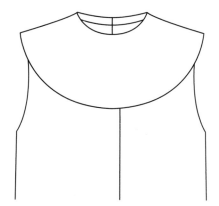
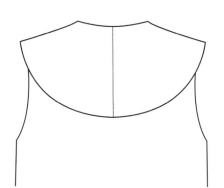

BOW/PUSSY BOW

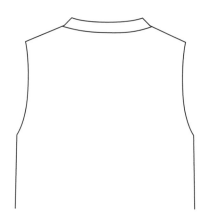

CASCADE/JABOT

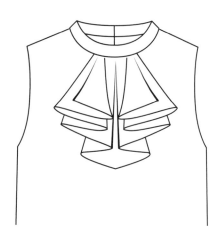
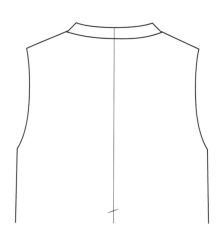

Collars

PURITAN/PILGRIM COLLAR

Front views   Back views

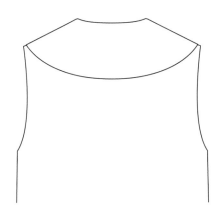

PIERROT COLLAR

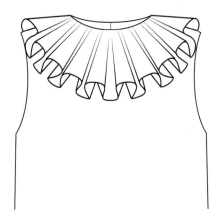

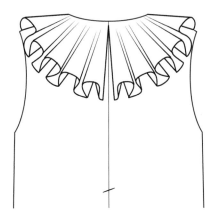

POLO COLLAR

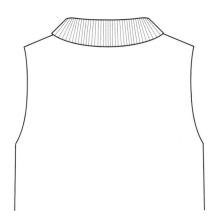

SET-IN SLEEVE
Front view

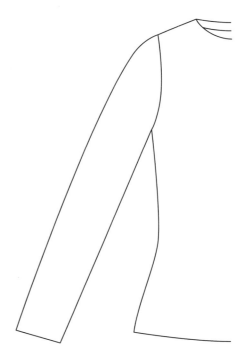

Back view

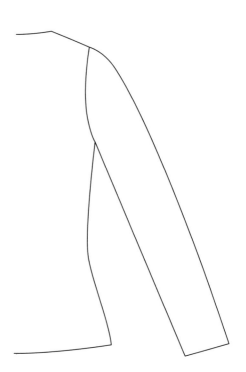

Sleeves

DROPPED SLEEVE/DROPPED SHOULDER
Front view

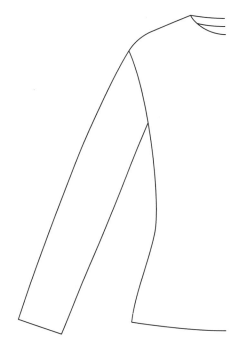

Back view

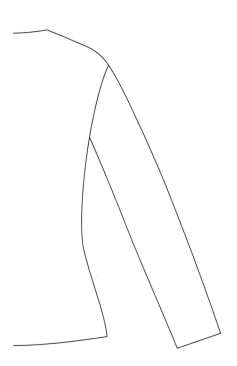

ONE-PIECE SLEEVE
Front view

 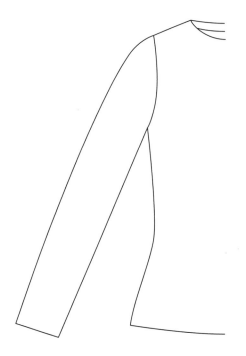

Back view

 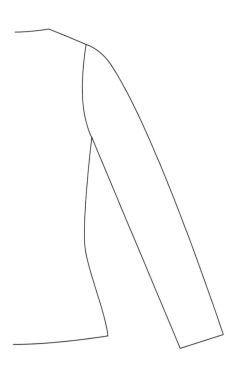

Sleeves

TWO-PIECE SLEEVE
Front view

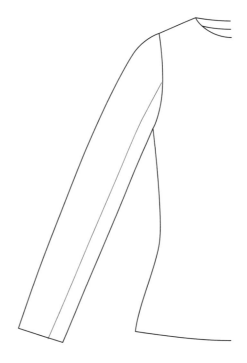

Back view

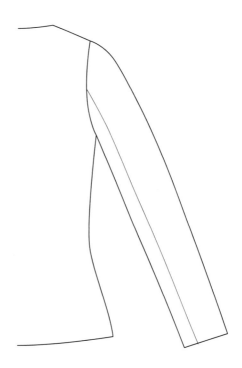

Sleeves

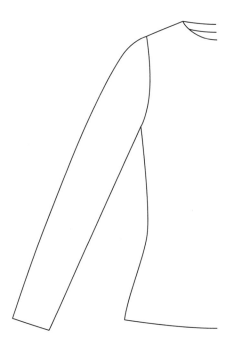 KEY BASIC SHAPES

FITTED SLEEVE
Front view

Back view

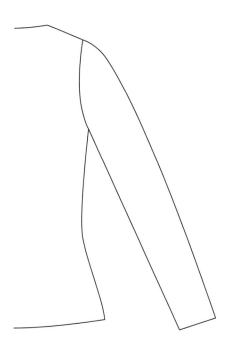

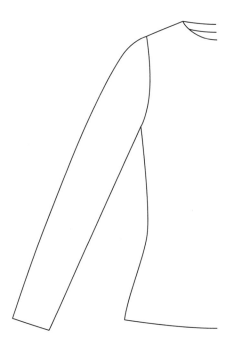

Sleeves

SHIRT SLEEVE
Front view

 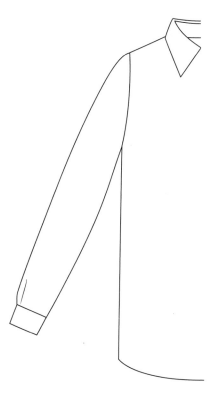

Back view

 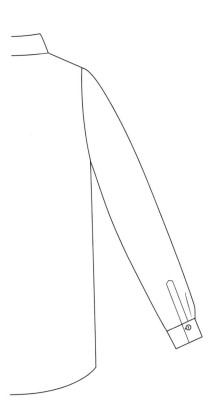

CAPPED SLEEVE
Front views

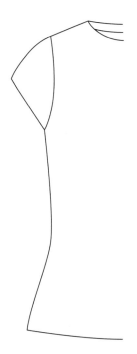

PUFF SLEEVE

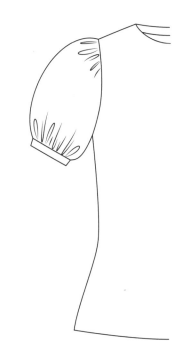

Back views

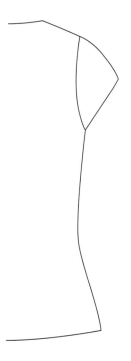

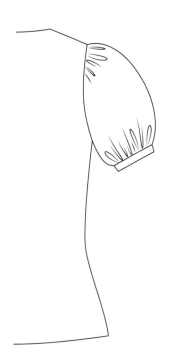

Sleeves

BELL SLEEVE
Front views

CAPE/FLARED/BUTTERFLY SLEEVE

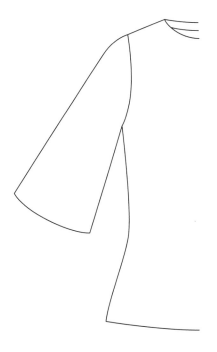

Back views

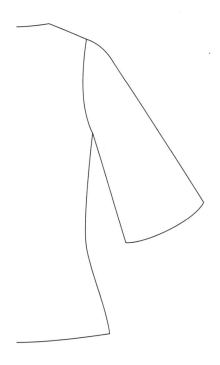

LANTERN SLEEVE
Front views

PAGODA SLEEVE

PEASANT SLEEVE

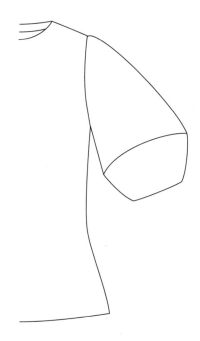 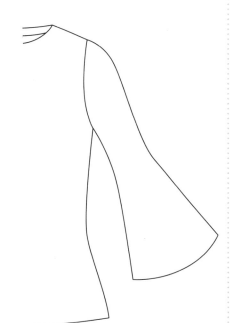 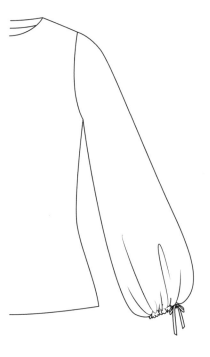

Back views

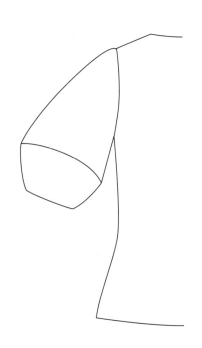 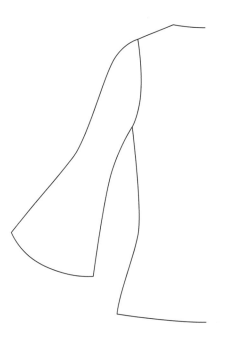 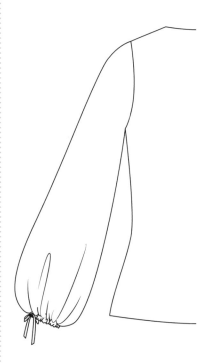

Sleeves

KIMONO SLEEVE
Front views

RAGLAN SLEEVE

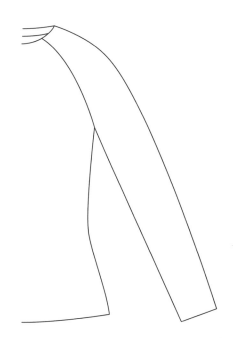

Back views

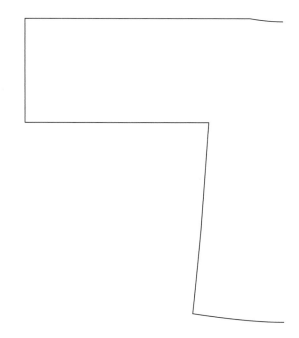

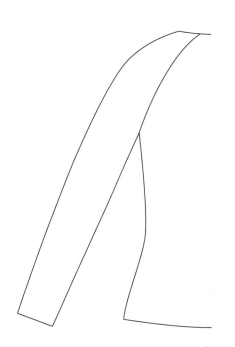

DOLMAN/MAGYAR SLEEVE/BATWING

Front views

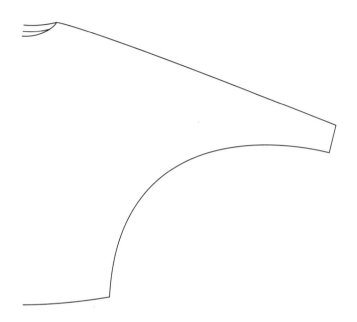

KITE SLEEVE

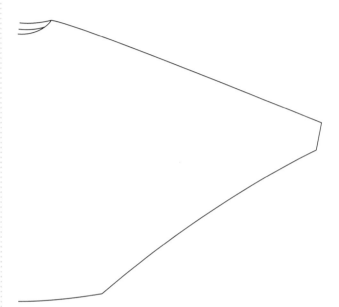

Back views

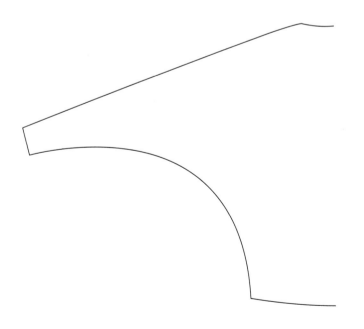

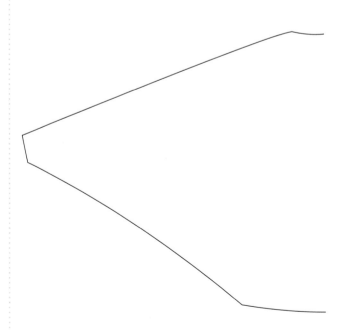

Sleeves

BISHOP SLEEVE
Front views

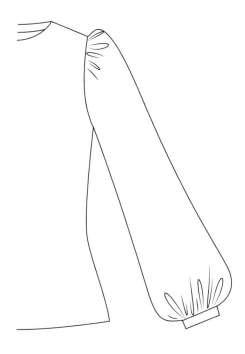

LEG-OF-MUTTON SLEEVE

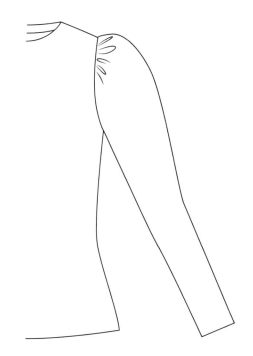

Back views

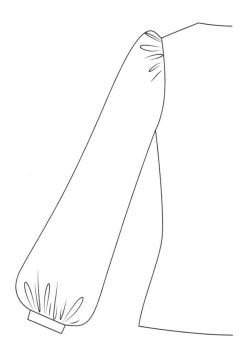

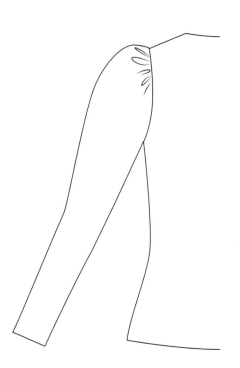

SINGLE/BARREL CUFF WITH PLACKET
Front views

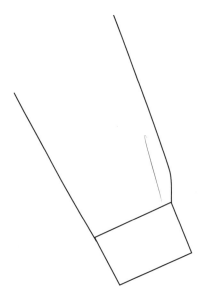

Back views

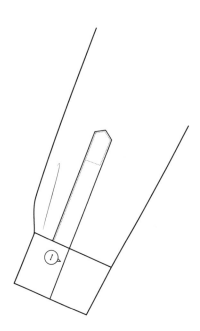

Cuffs

FRENCH CUFF
Front views

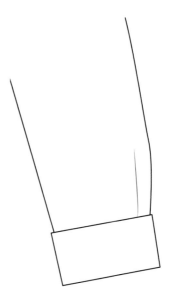

Back views

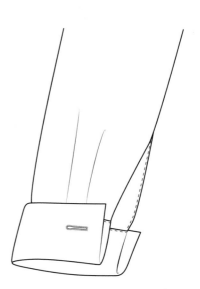

BOUND CUFF

Front view

Back view

Cuffs

DRAWSTRING CUFF

Front view

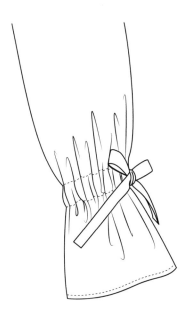

Back view

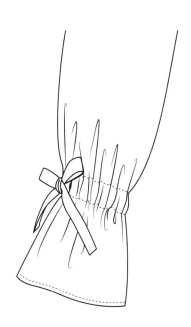

CREW NECK/SWEATER
Front views

CREW NECK (RAGLAN) SWEATER

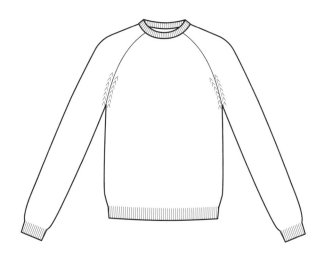

Back views

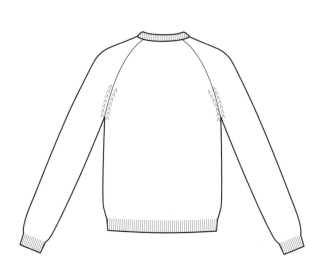

Knitwear

V-NECK (MITRED) SWEATER
Front views

SHORT-SLEEVED SWEATER

Back views

TWIN SET
Front views

Back views

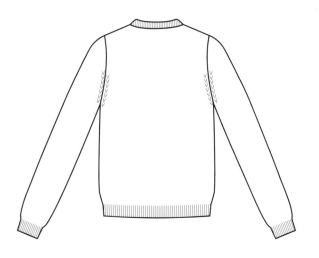

Knitwear

V-NECK CARDIGAN
Front views

V-NECK CARDIGAN WITH CABLE

Back views

SHAWL-COLLAR SWEATER
Front views

SQUARE SHAWL-COLLAR SWEATER

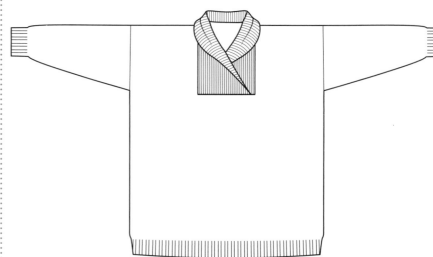

Back views

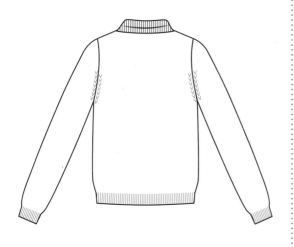

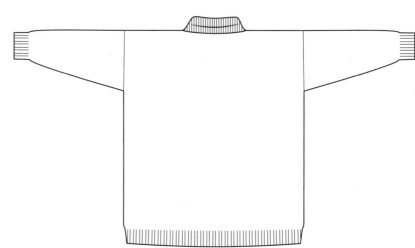

Knitwear

SQUARE SLASH-NECK SWEATER

Front views

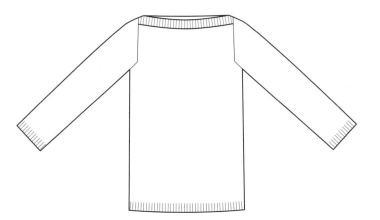

Back views

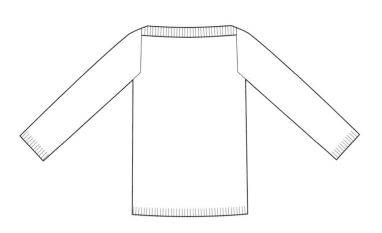

FUNNEL-NECK SWEATER

NOTCHED-NECK TUNIC
Front views

DOLMAN SWEATER

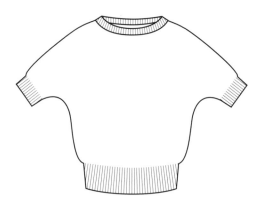

Back views

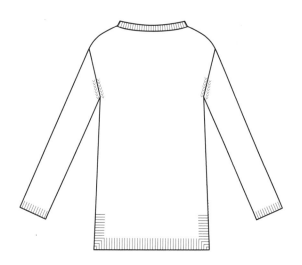

DRAPED/WATERFALL CARDIGAN (CLOSED)
Front views

DRAPED/WATERFALL CARDIGAN (OPEN)

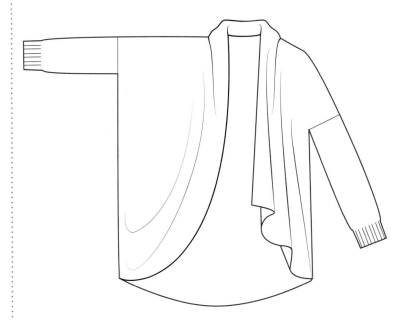

Back views

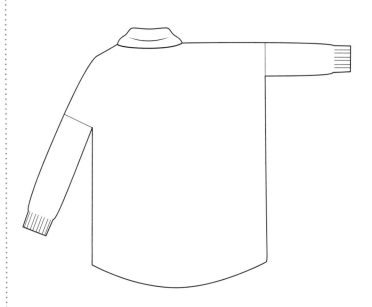

CIRCLE CARDIGAN
Front views

SWEATER COAT/LONG CARDIGAN

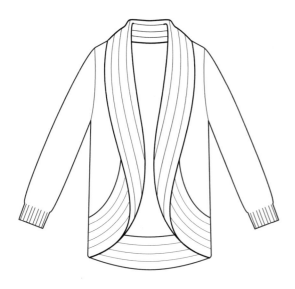

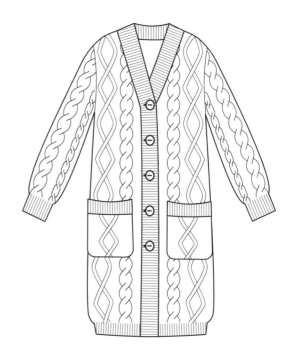

Back views

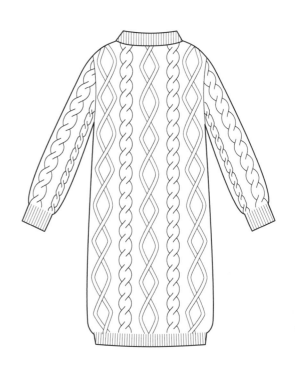

Knitwear

SPORTS CARDIGAN (TEXTURED)
Front views

HOODED SWEATER/HOODIE

Back views

V-NECK TANK TOP
Front views

TANK TOP (ARGYLE)

Back views

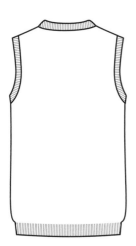

Knitwear

KIMONO SWEATER
Front views

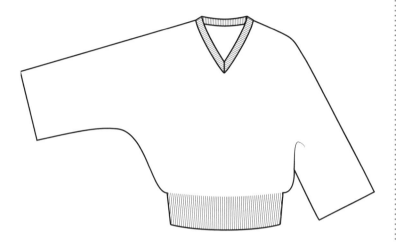

CAPELET/SHORT PONCHO

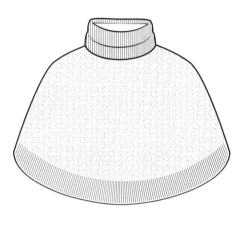

Back views

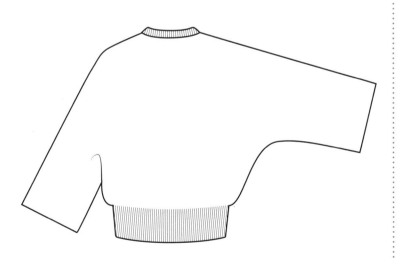

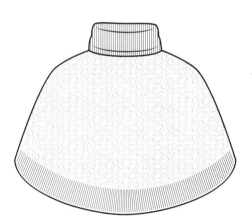

PONCHO (ROUND HEM)
Front views

PONCHO (TRIANGLE HEM)

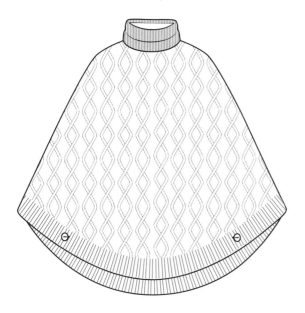

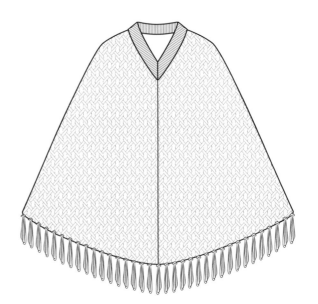

Back views

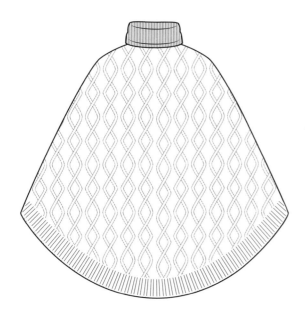

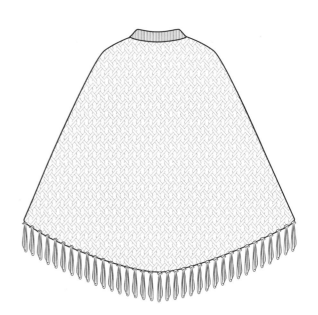

BASIC CUT-AND-SEWN SLEEVE
Front views

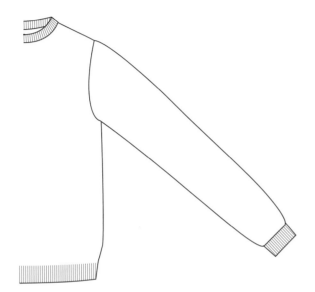

RAGLAN CUT-AND-SEWN SLEEVE

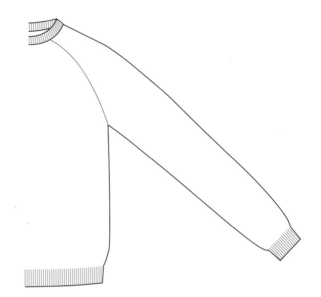

Back views

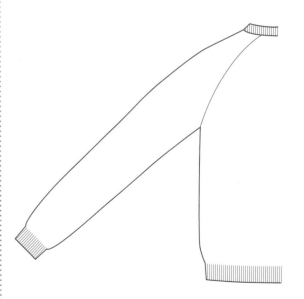

DROPPED-SHOULDER SLEEVE
Front views

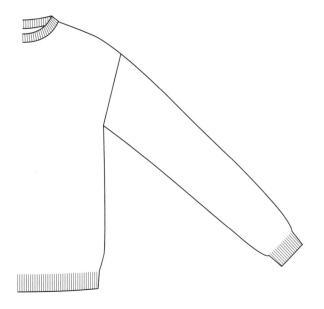

RAGLAN FULLY-FASHIONED SLEEVE

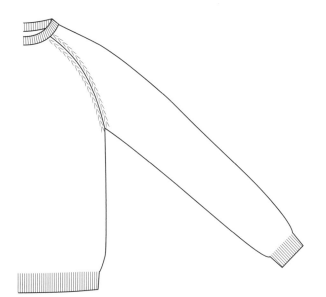

Back views

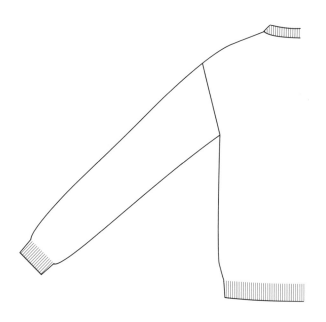

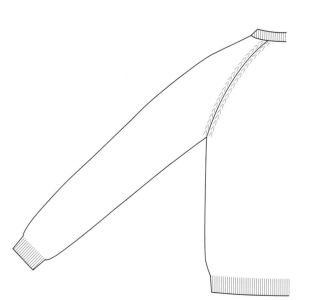

Knitwear

SADDLE-SHOULDER SLEEVE

Front views

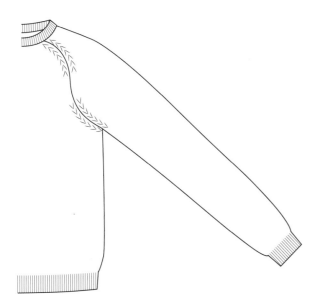

SEMI FULLY-FASHIONED SLEEVE

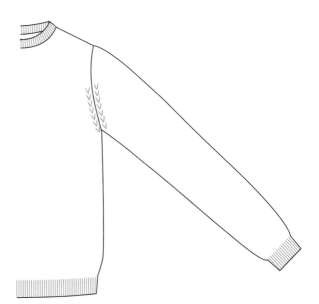

Back views

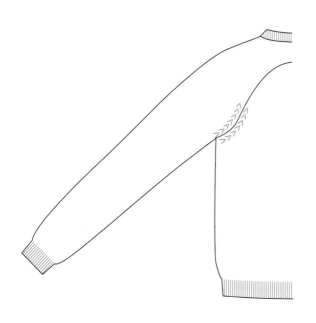

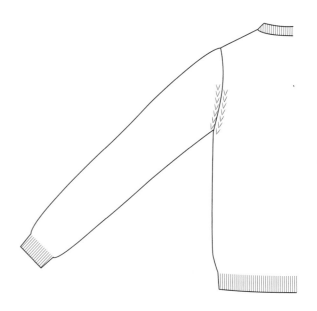

SQUARE SLEEVE
Front view

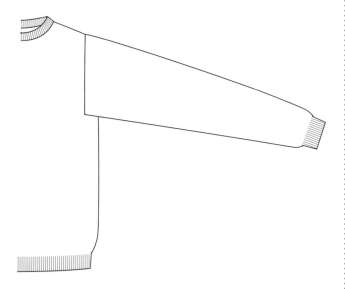

HIGH OR TALL RIB

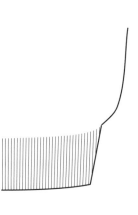

Back view

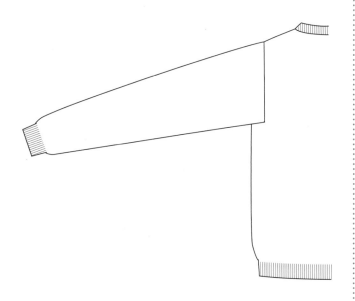

2X2 RIB

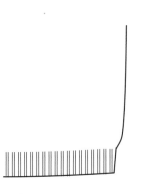

SHORT OR LOW RIB 3X3

1X1 RIB

3X3 RIB

4X4 RIB

PATCH POCKET

FLAP POCKET

WELT/JETTED/PIPED/BESOM POCKET

Details

BELLOWS/CARGO/SAFARI POCKET

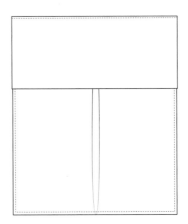

IN-A-SEAM POCKET (EXTERNAL VIEW)

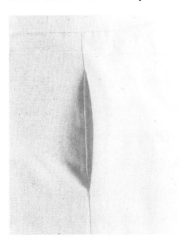
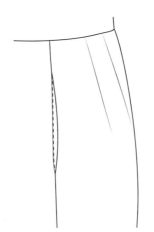

IN-A-SEAM POCKET (INTERNAL VIEW)

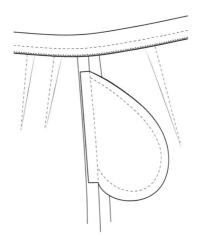

DART

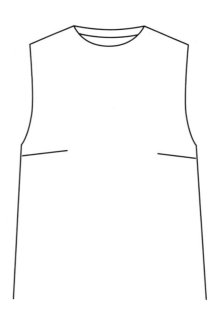

TUCK

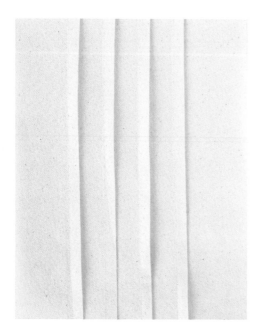

Details

GATHERS

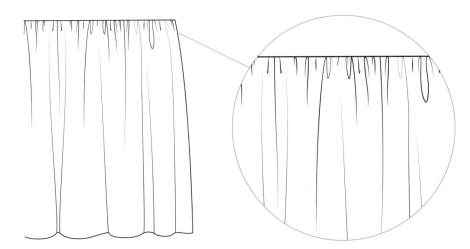

GUSSET

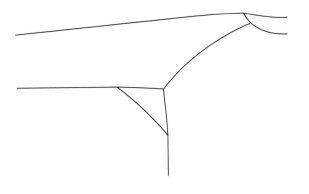

YOKE
Front view   Back view

BINDING

MITER

Front view

Back view

 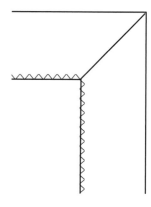

ROLLED HEM

Details

INSEAM

Front view

Back view

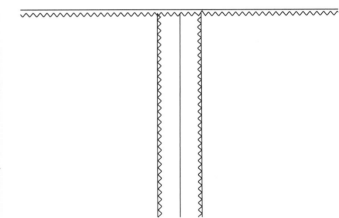

FRAYED EDGE

Details

PIPING

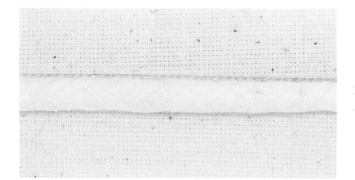

RUFFLE/FRILL

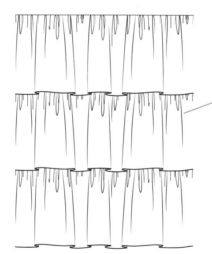

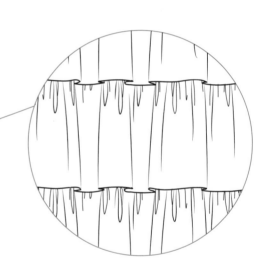

TAB CUFF

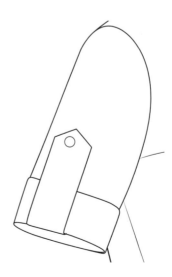

Details

PLACKET

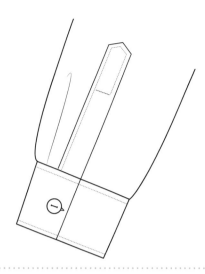

CONCEALED PLACKET

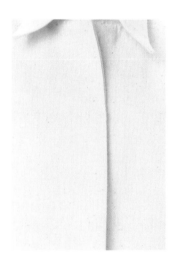

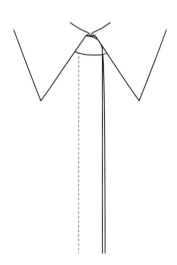

BELT LOOP

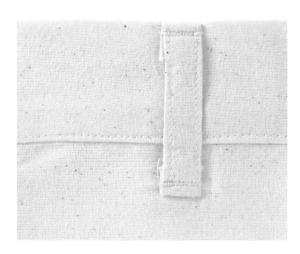

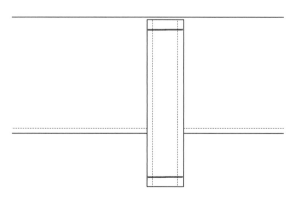

COLLAR STAND

Front view

Back view

ZIPPED FLY

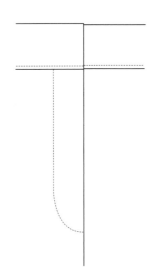

UNZIPPED FLY

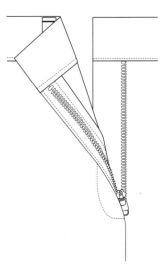

GODET

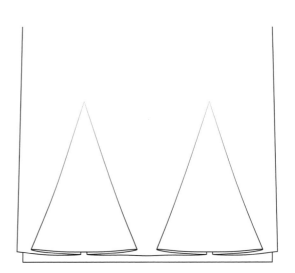

Details

SLIT

 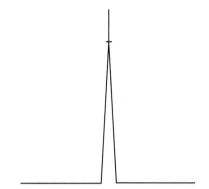

EPAULETTE

 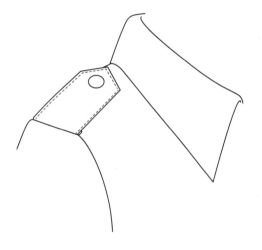

RIB (1)

 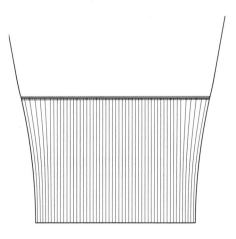

RIB (2)

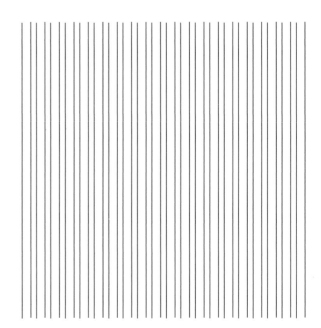

RIB (3)

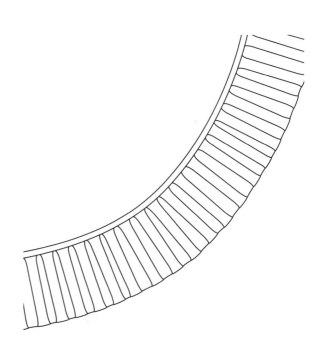

Details

CUFF

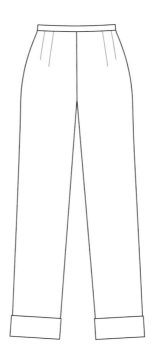

HOOD

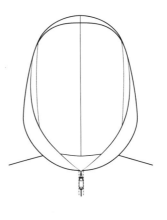

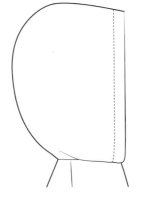

RUCHING

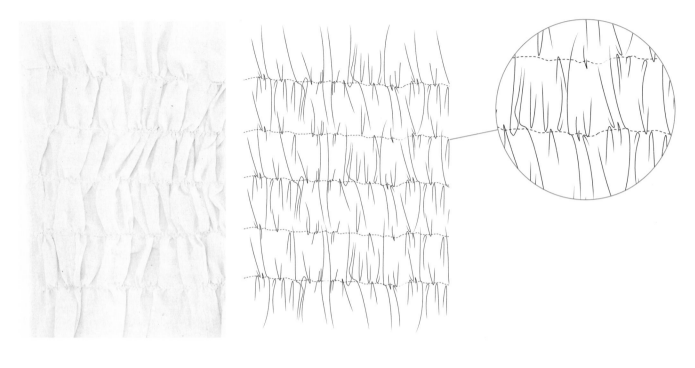

SMOCKING

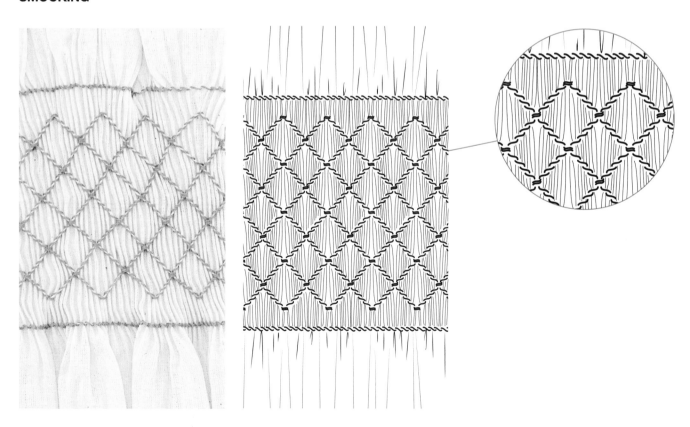

Details

SCALLOP

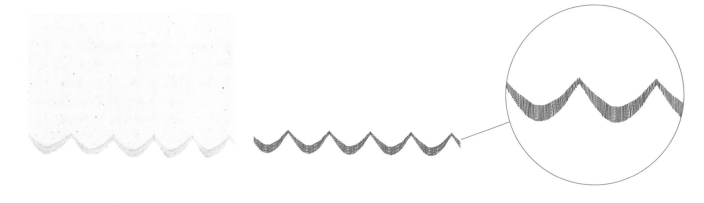

SHIRRING

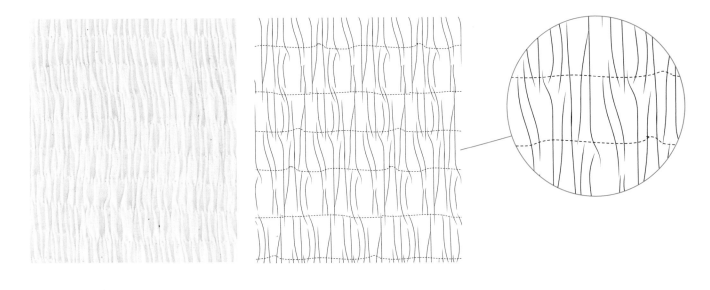

QUILTING

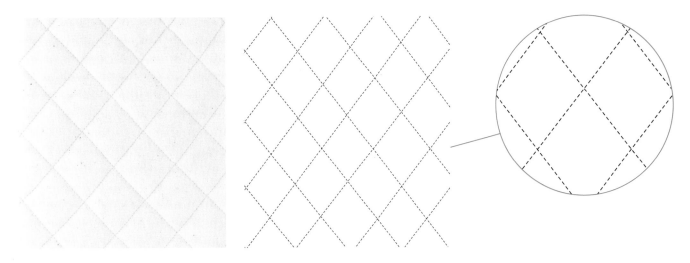

APPLIQUE

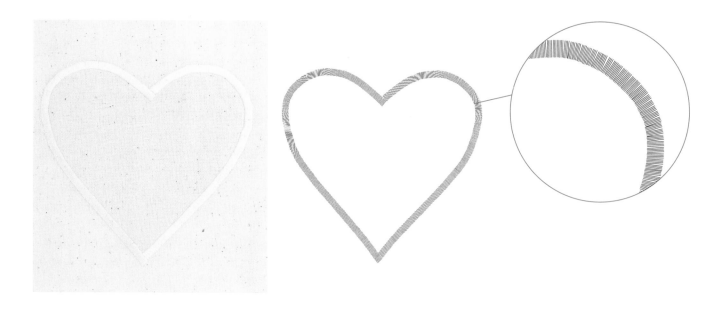

TASSEL

Details

FRINGE

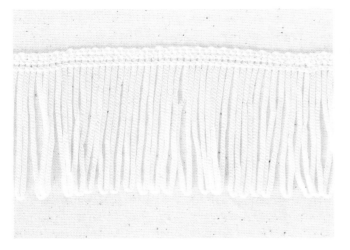
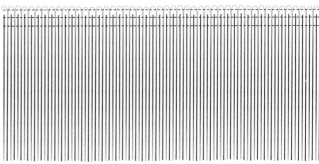

POM POM

Details

ACCORDION PLEAT

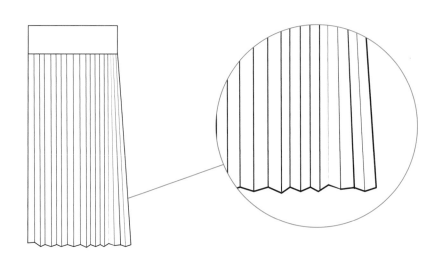

KNIFE PLEAT

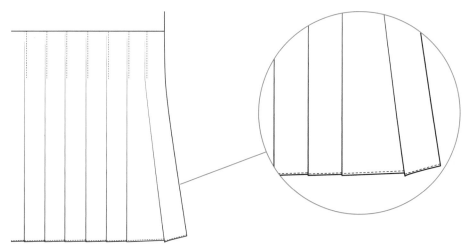

BOX PLEAT

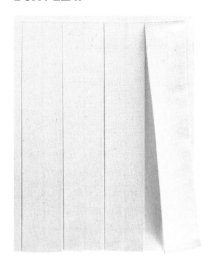
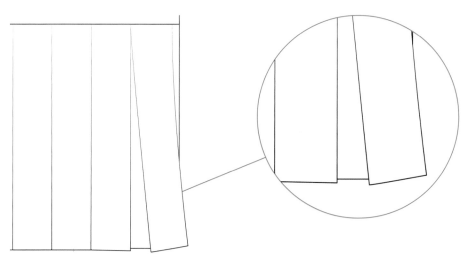

Details

INVERTED PLEAT

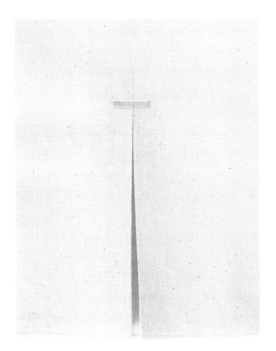

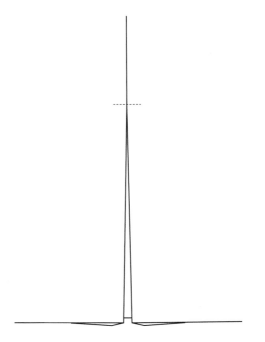

KICK PLEAT

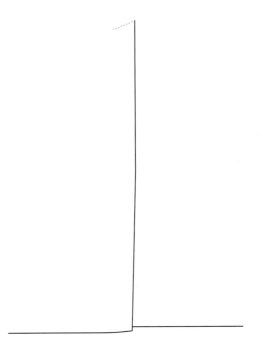

TOP STITCH/RUNNING STITCH (SINGLE ROW)

TOP STITCH/RUNNING STITCH (DOUBLE ROW)

Details

FLAT FELL/TWIN NEEDLE

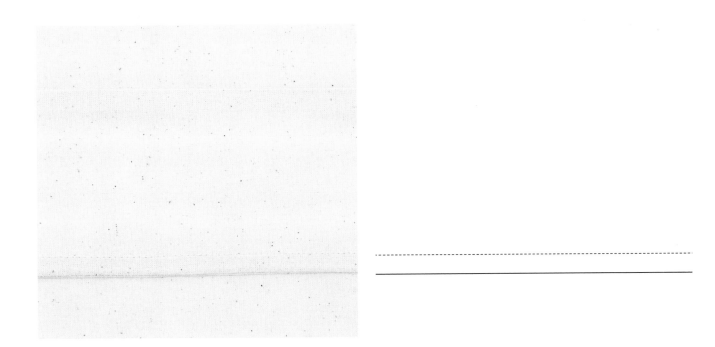

FRENCH SEAM

BOUND SEAM

EDGE STITCH

Details

LAPPED SEAM

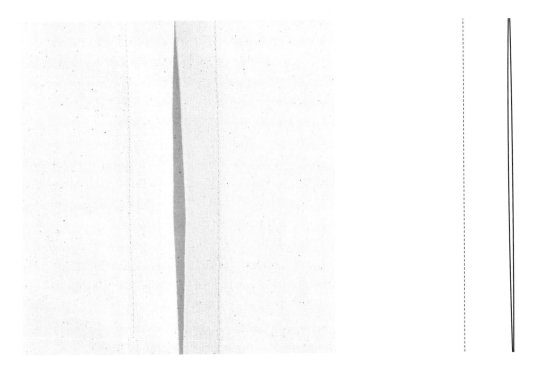

CHANNEL/SLOT SEAM

STRAIGHT LOCKSTITCH

TWIN NEEDLE

ZIG ZAG

Details

OVERLOCKING

BLIND STITCH/HEM STITCH

BLANKET STITCH

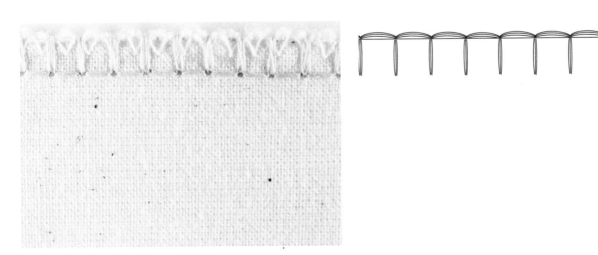

CROSS STITCH

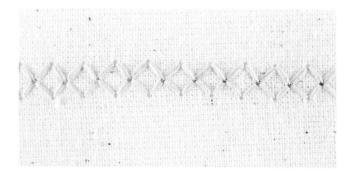

CHAIN STITCH

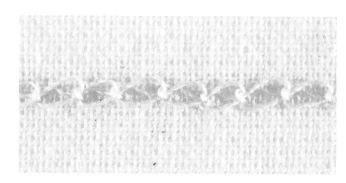

BAR TACK

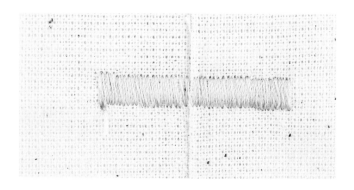
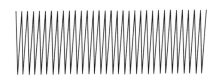

FOUR-HOLE BUTTON

 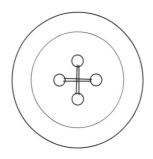

TWO-HOLE BUTTON

 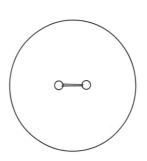

COVERED BUTTON/SHANK BUTTON

 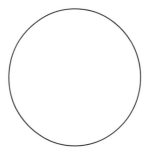

POPPER/PRESS STUD/SNAP

HOOK & LOOP (UNDONE)

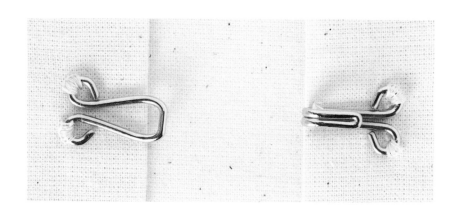 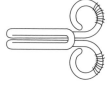

HOOK & LOOP (DONE UP)

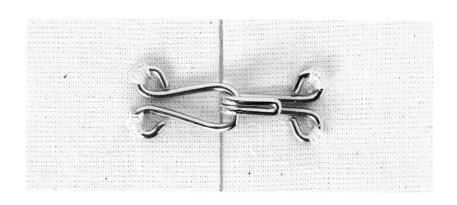 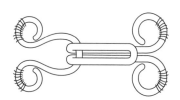

Details

TIE (UNTIED)

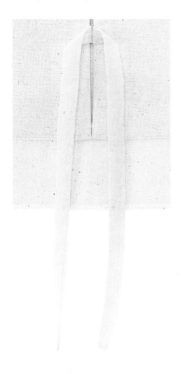

TIE (TIED IN A BOW)

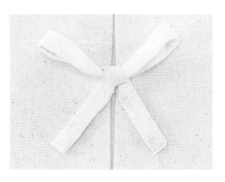

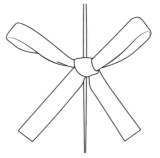

CHINESE KNOT

TOGGLE

FROGS/FROGGING

ROULEAU/BUTTON AND LOOP

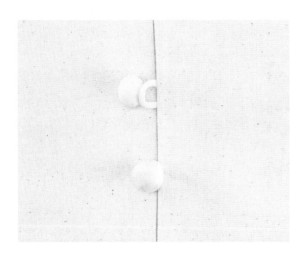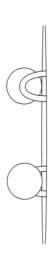

MACHINED BUTTONHOLE

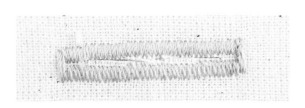

Details

KEYHOLE

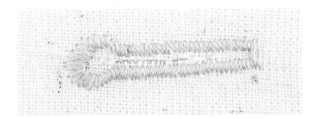

BOUND BUTTONHOLE

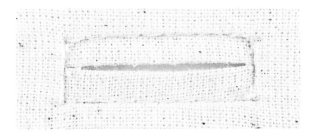

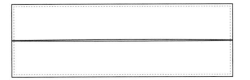

INVISIBLE ZIPPER

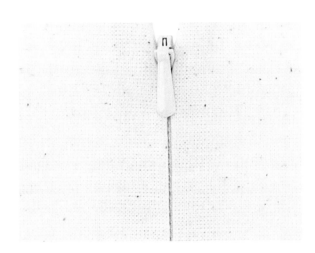

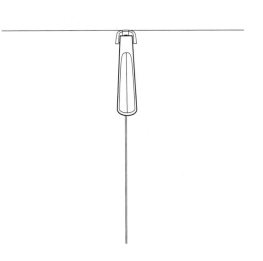

VISIBLE ZIPPER

 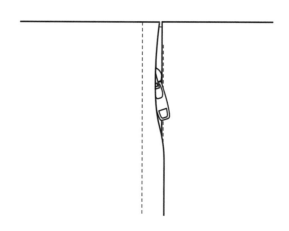

TWO-WAY ZIPPER

 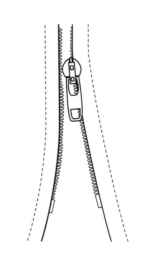

VELCRO

 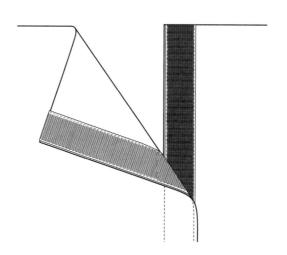

Details

EYELETS/GROMMETS

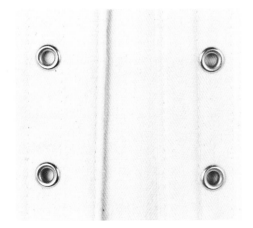
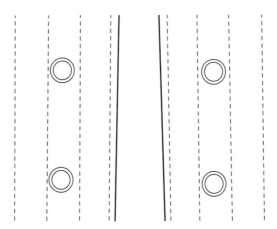

LACING

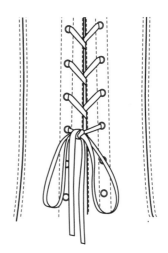

STUD

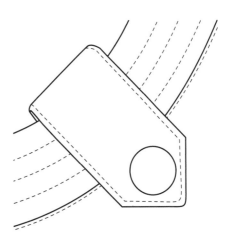

RIVET

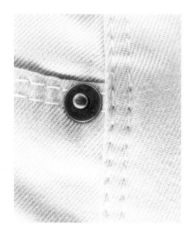

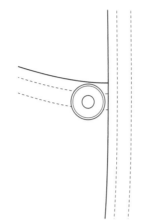

D-RING

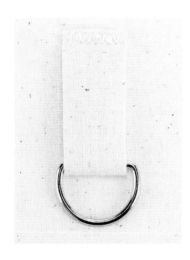

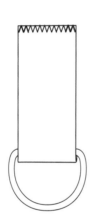

BUCKLE

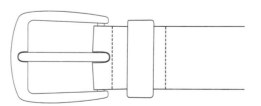

DRAWSTRING TOGGLE

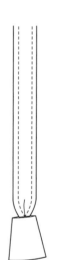

GLOSSARY, INDEX, & RESOURCES

Glossary

A

A-line Garment that flares out from shoulder or waist to hem, like the letter "A."

Apparel Generic term for clothing.

Asymmetric Garments or details that are different in proportion on the right-hand side from the left.

C

CAD Computer-aided design.

Center-line Vertical line drawn down the middle of a sheet of paper as the starting point for a technical drawing template.

Collar Stand Band of material attached to the neckline of a garment to support the collar.

Coloring-up Rendering a drawing to show color, texture, or pattern.

Colorway One of a range of colors or color combinations used to create a garment.

Costing Sheet List of all the elements needed to make up a garment (fabric, trims, cost of manufacture), which is then used to calculate the manufacturing, gross margin and selling price of a style.

D

Dart Tapered tuck stitched into a garment in order to fit it to the body.

Double-breasted Garment, usually a coat or jacket, with a wide overlap at the font, wrapping over the chest and fastening with buttons. Two rows of button are visible when closed.

F

Flats Technical drawings created to give an accurate representation of a garment. Also called "working drawings" or "line drawings."

Floats Technical drawings that have been embellished with color or pattern.

Frogging Braided or corded decorative fastening.

G

Godet Triangular piece of fabric inserted into a garment to add fullness.

Gusset Triangular or diamond-shaped piece of fabric inserted into a garment to reinforce or expand a part of it. Often used under the arm or at the crotch.

H

Hardware The–traditionally metal–closures, fixings, and decorative additions on a garment.

L

Lapel One of two triangular flaps below the collar, pressed back to the chest, on jackets, coats and shirts.

Light Box Table-top box, usually made from acrylic, that is illuminated from the rear, assisting with tracing and design work.

Line Board Presentation of a collection of co-ordinating garment styles showing individual styles and colorways.

Line Sheet Sales document presenting information such as style, colors, fabrics, order quantities, delivery period, manufacturing, and selling prices along with garment sketches to wholesale buyers.

Look Book Designers' or manufacturers' portfolio presenting a season's line; can include flats, catwalk shots, and illustrations.

M

Mannequin Dummy of the human body used to display clothing.

Merchandising Plan Graphic representation of a store floor area in 2D or 3D used to plan the display of garments prior to the collection arriving in store.

Muslin Trial garment created during the early design stages so the garment can be seen three-dimensionally and fit and drape assessed. Usually made in cotton or a cloth that replicates the final intended fabric.

O

Outerwear Garments designed to be worn over the top of other items of clothing.

P

Placket Opening in a garment that allows the wearer to put it on. Usually positioned at the waist, collar, cuffs, and neck of a garment.

Plan View Head-on perspective view of a garment.

Plus Size Clothing made especially for a larger body that goes beyond the traditional range of sizes.

Princess Line Garment, usually a women's coat, which is fitted at the waist, and flares out toward the hem.

R

Rever Wide lapel that is turned back to show the reverse side.

Rivet Type of metal fastener used in garment construction.

S

Set-in Refers to part of a garment that has been inserted, e.g. a sleeve that has been sewn into an armhole rather than cut as part of the bodice.

Sketch Rough, spontaneous drawing of a garment idea that is not necessarily accurate or in proportion.

Specification Sheet (or "spec") Includes a technical drawing (including front and back views and, if necessary, a side view and internal views), plus all detailed measurements required to produce the garment.

Speed Designing A shortcut to producing technical drawings. Once a garment style has been drawn using the generic template, that style can then be used as a template for developing any number of variations. Facilitates the drawing of real working garments, rather than just sketching out rough ideas.

Slit An opening in a garment to allow for ventilation or ease of movement.

T

Technical Drawing The process of creating flats, also known as "working drawings" or "line drawings." Technical drawings are an accurate representation of a garment.

Trend Books Industry publications that can contain mood boards, fabric swatches, illustrations, and flats, intended to provide a forecast of new ideas for future seasons.

W

Welt Border used to decorate or reinforce part of a garment, such as a pocket or seam.

Y

Yoke A fitted piece of fabric, usually across the shoulders (in shirts, coats, etc) or hips (in skirts and pants), to which the rest of the garment is attached.

Useful professional organizations

EUROPE

UK

British Apparel and Textile Confederation (BATC)
5 Portland Place, London W1N 3AA
Tel: +44 (0)20 7636 7788
Fax: +44 (0)20 7636 7515
Email: batc@dial.pipex.com
Website: www.batc.co.uk

British Clothing Industry Association (BCIA)
5 Portland Place, London W1B 1PW
Tel: +44 (0)20 7636 7788 or +44 (0)20 7636 5577
Fax: +44 (0) 20 7636 7515
Email: contact@5portlandplace.org.uk
Website: www.5portlandplace.org.uk

British Fashion Council (BFC)
5 Portland Place, London W1B 1PW
Tel: + 44 (0)20 7636 7788
Fax: +44 (0)20 7436 5924
Email: emmacampbell@britishfashioncouncil.com
www.britishfashioncouncil.com

EMTEX LTD (Designer Forum)
69–73 Lower Parliament Street,
   Nottingham NG1 3BB
Tel: +44 (0)115 9115339
Fax: +44 (0) 115 911 5345
Email: info@design-online.net
Website: www.design-online.net

Fashion and Design Protection Association Ltd.
69 Lawrence Road, London N15 4EY
Tel: +44 (0)20 8800 5777
Fax: +44 (0)20 8880 2882
Email: info@fdpa.co.uk
Website: www.fdpa.co.uk

Northern Ireland Textile and Apparel Assoc. Ltd.
5c The Square, Hillsborough BT26 6AG
Tel: +44 (0)2892 68 9999
Fax: +44 (0)2892 68 9968
Email: info@nita.co.uk

Register of Apparel & Textile Designers
5 Portland Place, London W1N 3AA
Tel: +44 (0)20 7636 5577
Fax: +(44) (0)20 7436 5924
Email: contact@5portlandplace.org.uk
Website: www.5portlandplace.org.uk

France

Chambre Syndicale de la Couture Parisienne
45 Rue Saint-Roch, 75001 Paris
Tel: + 33 (0)1 4261 0077
Fax: +33 (0)1 4286 8942
Email: ecole@modeaparis.com
Website: www.modeaparis.com

Fédération Francaise du Prêt-à-Porter Féminine
5 Rue Caumartin, 75009 Paris
Tel: +33 (0)1 4494 7030
Fax: +33 (0)1 4494 7004
Email: contact@pretparis.com
Website: www.pretaporter.com

Fédération Française des Industries du
   Vêtement Masculin
8 Rue Montesquieu, 75001 Paris
Tel. : +33 (0)1 44 55 66 50
Fax : +33 (0)1 44 55 66 65
Website: www.lamodefrancais.org.fr

Germany

Confederation of the German Textile
   and Fashion Industry
Frankfurter Strasse 10–14, D-65760 Eschborn
Tel: +49 6196 9660
Fax: +49 6196 42170
Email: info@textil-mode.de
Website: www.textil-mode.de

Italy

Associazione Italiana della Filiera Tessile
   Abbigliamento SMI
Federazione Tessile e Moda
Viale Sarca 223, 20126 Milano
Tel: +39 (0)2-641191
Fax: +39 (0)2-66103667 / 70
Website: www.smi-ati.it
Email: info@sistemamodaitalia.it

Centro di Firenze per la Moda Italiana
Via Faenzan, 111, 50123, Florence
Tel: +39 (0)553 6931
Fax: +39 (0)5536 93200
Email: cfmi@cfmi.it
Website: www.cfmi.it

Spain

Association of New and Young Spanish Designers
Segovia 22, Bajos CP 28005 Madrid
Tel: +34 915 475 857
Fax: +34 915 475 857
Website: www.nuevosde.com
Email: nuevosdisenadores@telefonica.net

ASIA AND THE PACIFIC

Australia

Council of Textiles and Fashion Industries,
   Australia Ltd (TFIA)
Level 2, 20 Queens Road, Melbourne, VIC 3004
Tel: +61 (0) 38317 6666
Fax: +61 (0) 38317 6666
Email: info@tfia.com.au
Website: www.tfia.com.au

Design Institute of Australia
486 Albert Street, East Melbourne, VIC 3002,
   GPO Box 4352
Tel: +61 (0) 38662 5490
Fax: +61 (0) 38662 5358
Email: admin@design.org.au
Website: www.dia.org.au

Australian Fashion Council
Showroom 16, 23–25 Gipps Street,
   Collingwood VIC 3066
Tel: +61 (0) 38680 9400
Fax: +61 (0) 38680 9499
Email: info@australianfashioncouncil.com
Website: www.australianfashioncouncil.com

Melbourne Design and Fashion Incubator (MDFI)
Shop 238, Level 2, Central Shopping Centre, 211
   La Trobe Street, Melbourne 3000, Victoria
Tel: +61 (0) 39671 4522
Email: info@fashionincubator.com.au
Website: www.fashionincubator.com.au

China

China National Textile and Apparel Council
China Textile Network Company, Rm 236, No 12,
   Dong Chang'an Street, Beijing 100742

Tel: +86 10 85229 100
Fax: +86 10 85229 100
Email: einfo@ml.ctei.gov.cn
Website: www.ctei.gov.cn

China Fashion Designers Association
Room 154, No 12, Dong Chang'an Street,
   Beijing, 100742
Tel: +86 1085 229427
Fax: +86 1085 229037

Japan

Japan Fashion Association
Fukushima Building, 1-5-3 Nihonbashi –
   Muromachi, Chuo – ku, Tokyo, 103-0022
Tel: +81 33242 1677
Fax: +81 33242 1678
Email: info@japanfashion.or.jp
Website: japanfashion.or.jp

Japan Association of Specialist in Textile
   and Apparel
Jasta Office, 2-11-13-205, Shiba – koen,
   Minato – Ku, Toyko 105-0011
Tel: +81 03 3437 6416
Fax: +81 03 3437 3194
Email: jasta@mtb.biglobe.ne.jp
Website: jasta1.or.jp/index_english.html

NORTH AMERICA

USA

American Apparel and Footwear Association
1601 N Kent Street, Suite 1200, Arlington VA
   22209
Tel: +1 703 524 1864
Fax: +1 703 522 6741
Website: www.apparelandfootwear.org

Council of Fashion Designers of America
1412 Broadway Suite 2006, New York 10018
Tel: +1 212 302 1821
Website: www.cfda.com

Fashion Group International New York
8 West 40th Street, 7th Floor, New York NY10018
Tel: +1 212 302 5511
Fax: +1 212 302 5533
Email: e-cheryl@fgi.org
Website: www.fgi.org

International Textile and Apparel Association
ITAA 6060 Sunrise Vista Drive, Suite 1300,
   Citrus Heights, CA 95610
Tel: +1 916 723 1628
Email: info@itaaonline.org
Website: www.itaaonline.org

Brazilian–American Fashion Association
   (BRAMFSA)
PO Box 83-2036, Delray Brach, Florida 33483
Website: www.bramfsa.com

Canada

Canadian Apparel Federation
124 O'Connor Street, Suite 504, Ottawa, Ontario
   K1P 5M9
Tel: +1 613 231 3220
Fax: +1 613 231 2305
Email: info@apparel.ca
Website: www.apparel.ca

Index

Further reading & credits

FURTHER READNG

Abling, Bina and Kathleen Maggio, *Integrating Draping, Drafting and Drawing*, Fairchild, 2008

Centner, Marianne, and Frances Vereker, *Adobe Illustrator: A Fashion Designer's Handbook*, Blackwell, 2007

Aldrich, Winifred, *Metric Pattern Cutting for Children's Wear and Babywear*, Blackwell Publishing, 4th edition, 2009

Aldrich, Winifred, *Metric Pattern Cutting for Menswear, Blackwell Publishing*, 4th edition, 2008

Aldrich, Winifred, *Metric Pattern Cutting for Womenswear*, Blackwell Publishing, 5th edition, 2008

Armstrong, Helen Joseph, *Patternmaking for Fashion Design*, Pearson Education, 4th edition, 2005

Bray, Natalie, *Dress Pattern Designing*, Blackwell Publishing, 2003

Burke, Sandra, *Fashion Artist: Drawing Techniques to Portfolio Presentation*, Burke Publishing, 2nd edition, 2006

Burke, Sandra, *Fashion Computing - Design Techniques and CAD*, Burke Publishing, 2006

Campbell, Hilary, *Designing Patterns - A Fresh Approach to Pattern Cutting*, Nelson Thornes, 1980

Cooklin, Gerry, *Garment Technology for Fashion Designers*, Blackwell, 1997

Cooklin, Gerry, *Pattern Cutting for Women's Outerwear*, OM Books, 2008

Fischer, Annette, *Basics Fashion Design: Construction*, AVA Publishing SA, 2009

Ireland, Patrick John, *New Encyclopedia Of Fashion Details*, B T Batsford Ltd, 2008

Knowles, Lori A, *The Practical Guide To Patternmaking For Fashion Designers: Menswear*, Fairchild, 2005

Knowles, Lori A, *The Practical Guide To Patternmaking For Fashion Designers: Juniors, Misses, And Women*, Fairchild, 2005

Lazear, Susan, *Adobe Illustrator for Fashion Design*, Prentice Hall, 2008

Lazear, Susan, *Adobe Photoshop for Fashion Design*, Prentice Hall, 2009

McKelvey, Kathryn, *Fashion Source Book*, Blackwell; 2nd Edition, 2006

Peacock, John, *The Complete Fashion Sourcebook: 2,000 Illustrations Charting 20th-Century Fashion*, Thames & Hudson, 2005

Renfrew, Elinor, *Developing a Fashion Collection* (Basics Fashion Design), Fairchild, 2nd revised edition, 2016

Riegelman, Nancy, *9 Heads: A Guide to Drawing Fashion*, Prentice Hall, 3rd edition, 2006

Rosen, Sylvia, *Patternmaking: A Comprehensive Reference for Fashion Design*, Prentice Hall, 2004

Seivewright, Simon, *Basics Fashion Design: Research and Design*, AVA Publishing SA, 2007

Stipelman, Steven, *Illustrating Fashion: Concept To Creation*, Fairchild, 2nd edition, 2005

Tallon, Kevin, *Creative Computer Fashion Design with Illustrator*, 2006

Travers-Spencer, Simon, and Zarida Zaman, *The Fashion Designer's Directory of Shape and Style*, Barron's Educational Series, 2008

Ward, Janet, *Pattern Cutting and Making Up: The Professional Approach*, 2nd edition, Butterworth-Heinemann, 1987

PHOTO CREDITS

The authors and publisher would like to thank the following institutions and individuals who provided images for use in this book. In all cases, every effort has been made to credit the copyright holders, but should there be any omissions or errors the publisher would be pleased to insert the appropriate acknowledgment in any subsequent edition of this book.
p11 Ana Stankovic-Fitzgerald
p12 Wayne Fitzell
p13 (top) Wayne Fitzell; (bottom) Debenhams
p14 Look Book images, Patrick Lee Yow, spec sheet Kevan Tomlin
p15 Toby Meadows
p16 FashionSnoops www.fashionsnoops.com
p17 (top) Senso Group; (bottom) Ana Stankovic-Fitzgerald
p18 & 19 Vogue Patterns, courtesy of McCall, Butterick & Vogue
p20–25 Ana Stankovic-Fitzgerald
p26–27 Photography by PSC Photography Ltd.
p32–53 Tutorials by Ana Stankovic-Fitzgerald
54–65 Ana Stankovic-Fitzgerald
p66 (left) Vanda Rulewska; (right) Patrick Lee Yow
p67 (top) Mary Ruppert; (middle) Lynn Blake; (bottom) Elmaz Hüseyin
All technical drawings in section two by Ana Stankovic-Fitzgerald; All muslins produced by Ann Stafford and Ayako Koyama; all muslin photography by PSC Photography Ltd.

AUTHOR'S ACKNOWLEDGMENTS

I would like to especially thank my talented illustrator Ana Stankovic-Fitzgerald for working tirelessly with me to create all the flats in the book, as well as Anne Stafford and Ayako Koyama for creating all the impeccably constructed muslins. A big thank you to Kathryn Kujawa for supplying detailed information and research for the knits section, her expertise in this field is amazing—my knit "guru." Thank you to everyone that worked with me for your focus, dedication, and patience!

A special thank you to Eleanor Warrington for introducing me to the world of "flats" and commercial design so many years ago, in my first ever internship while still at St Martins: that's when fashion design was demystified for me, when I came to understand commercial design and when I realized that fashion design was a real career option and not just a fantasy.

I am also very grateful to all at Laurence King for working on this second edition to produce something that we believe is now perfect. Thank you to my patient and super-professional editors, Anne Townley and Gaynor Sermon—I have huge respect for you!

Basia would also like to thank the following individuals and organizations:
Jo Lightfoot
Anne Townley
Gaynor Sermon
Vanessa Green
Patrick Lee Yow
Wayne Fitzell
Vanda Rulewska
Sarah Bailey
Kevan Tomlin
Toby Meadows
Sean Chiles
Kathryn Kujawa
Polly Holman
Elmaz Hüseyin
Bridget Miles
Mary Ruppert-Stroescu
Lynn Blake
Keith Jones at McCall, Butterick & Vogue Patterns (www.butterick-vogue.co.uk)
Fashion Snoops (www.fashionsnoops.com)
Chloe Goodson and Sandra Ossei at Mode information
Kane Thompson and Ann-Louise Tingelof at Senso Group (www.sensogroup.co.uk)

AUTHOR'S DEDICATION

I dedicate this book to all students of any fashion-related discipline. Drawing is a language, and mastering the language of technical drawing can be of immense benefit to you. If you can draw, you can communicate. It looks difficult, but it's just a technique—which you will discover in this book. Practice makes perfect, don't be afraid to make mistakes, it's through making mistakes that we learn. Enjoy, have fun, and experiment. I've laid down the basics, now it's up to you to make this skill your own.